Making and Repairing Furniture

Making and Repairing Furniture

A Visual Guide

Klaus Pracht

B.T. Batsford Ltd · London

English translation © B.T. Batsford 1993
First published in English 1993

This work is a translation of the German book:
Möbel selber bauen und reparieren
von Klaus Pracht
published by AUGUSTUS VERLAG AUGSBURG
© 1990 Weltbild Verlag GmbH

Typeset by Servis Filmsetting Ltd,
Manchester
and printed in Great Britain by
The Bath Press, Bath

Published by B.T. Batsford Ltd
4 Fitzhardinge Street
London W1H 0AH

A CIP catalogue record for this book is
available from the British Library

ISBN 0 7134 7263 4

Foreword

There is a great deal of satisfaction to be gained from making and repairing your own furniture or redesigning it for a new function, and this comes easily when you enjoy the work and it is successful. The aim of this book is to help you achieve this.

While wood is a particularly versatile material from which to make your own furniture – it is reasonably priced and easy to work – both a basic and a detailed knowledge of making furniture (e.g. wood joints) remain essential for even the most skilled woodworker. Both are expertly shown in this book, aided by the use of clear diagrams.

The book is divided into four chapters, to make the information easily accessible:

Chapter 1 deals with the basics of making furniture. Working sketches and three dimensional drawings are necessary for the design as well as for the production of furniture, and it is important to recognize the functions of various pieces of furniture, e.g. whether or not joints are to be permanent. Furniture has to be designed and thought out – do you want hinged or sliding doors; are drawers to be suspended or will they slide open on runners? Frames have to be made stable, tables and chairs secured against tipping.

Chapter 2 is concerned with materials and wood joints, and draws attention to the differing treatment of naturally grown timber and manufactured board. You are shown how to make wood joints using both hand and small power tools.

Chapter 3 deals with repairing furniture. As often as not the reason for doing this comes from the pleasure one has from a particular piece of furniture, due to its design, quality or origin. Simple repairs are always cheaper than buying new furniture, and this book provides practical tips for the woodworker. Photos show the various types of repair: replacing shelves and sides; mending drawers, roll tops and doors; repairing dented and burnt areas and edges; and preventing tables and chairs from wobbling.

Chapter 4 deals with redesigning old furniture to give it a new lease of life. Often a piece of furniture can no longer be used in its original capacity, e.g. a washstand now superfluous in an age of bathrooms, and grandma's bed now long out of fashion; yet such old furniture is often too good to throw away – the material is usually first class and the design intricate.

Creative woodworkers will enjoy the challenge of making something worthwhile out of old pieces of furniture. Old and highly ornamental furniture may have simple, modern parts added, creating a tension between old and new, and intensifying the impact of the piece. Old box constructions may look quite different with a new coat of varnish or paint, but taking old pieces of furniture apart and rearranging the parts can have amazing results: chairs turn into chests, beds to benches and cupboard doors to display cabinets!

Repairing furniture is one thing, but reinventing it is another. With this book, an old or a plain piece of furniture can be turned into something special. I hope that you have a lot of fun – but don't forget to ask grandma first which pieces she is willing to part with.

Contents

1

Basic techniques

2

Furniture joints

3

Repairing
furniture

4

Breathing new
life into old
furniture

Planning and graphics 10
Planning 10
Graphics 10
Types of furniture 11
Construction plans 12

Cupboards 14
Parts 14
Construction methods 15
Knockdown fittings 16
Permanent joints 17

Doors 18
Hinged doors 18
Sliding doors 19
Hinges 20

Roll tops, flaps and lids 22
Roll tops 22
Flaps and lids 23
Flap fittings 24

Locks and catches 25
Locks 25
Catches 26
Knobs and handles 27

Drawers 28
Fitting drawers 28
Drawers on runners 29
Side-hung drawers 30

Shelves and stool-frame constructions 31
Free-standing shelves 31
Wall-mounted shelves 32
Stool-frame constructions 33

Tables and chairs 34
Tables 34
Chairs 35

Tools 38
Tools for measuring and marking out 38
Hand tools 39
Machine tools 40
Clamps and vices 41

Materials 42
Properties of wood 43
Commonly available prepared wood 44
Veneers and manufactured boards 45

Woodworking joints 46
Joints for widening boards and
    corner joints 46
Frame construction joints 47

Adhesives 48
Types of glue 48
Using adhesives 49

Halving 50
Cross halving 51

Bridle, mortise and tenon joints 52
Bridle joints 52
Mortise and tenon joints 53

Rebate joints 54

Tongue and groove joints 55

Dowel joints 56
Dowel joints without a jig 56
Using a dowelling jig 57

Comb and dovetail joints 58
Pin joints 59
Dovetails 60

Wedged joints 61
Glued wedges 61
Keyed joints 62

Screws and nails 63
Types 63
Using screws 64
Nailing 65

Metal fittings 66
Metal plates 66
Knockdown fittings 67

Fixing tops 70
Fitting shelves 72
Fitting central panels 73
Stabilizing shelves 74
Stabilizing furniture feet 76
Repairing drawer fronts and
    bottoms 78
Repairing drawer runners 80
Assembling roll tops and glueing
    battens 82

Fixing door frames and panels 84
Fitting single and continuous
    hinges 86
Removing and repairing pivot
    hinged doors 88
Fitting and improving bolts and
    locks 90
Regulating chair height and leg
    length 92
Fixing chair seats and frames 94

Fixing table tops 96
Repairing bed sides and joints 98
Fitting seats 100
Repairing edges 102
Strengthening shelves or boards 104
Removing dents and scratches 106
Removing burn and water marks 108
Fixing veneer edges 110
Restoring veneer surfaces 112

Old furniture – new function 116
From chair to table 116
From kitchen table to writing desk 116
From bed to table 117
From bed to shelf 117
From bed to cradle 118
From bed to seat 119
From cupboard parts to flights of
    fancy 120
From cupboard doors to display
    cabinet 122
Adding pieces to existing furniture 122
Interchanging cupboard halves 123

Sprucing up plain furniture 124
Adding to furniture 125
Sloping off corners 125
Moving furniture parts around 126
Changing angles 126

Techniques 127
Sections 127
Details 128

1 **Basic techniques**

KLAUS PRACHT · JENS BECKER

Introduction

Making furniture out of wood gives a special pleasure to many people since wood is so easy to work. The woodworker can put their own ideas into practice with satisfying results.

Planning
The following criteria are fundamental to good furniture design:
● the type and the size of the piece are determined by its function
● the construction should harmonize with the material and the form
● the design should include the proportions and dimensions as well as all visual aspects from texture to colour

Graphics   These can be anything from three-dimensional preliminary sketches and small scale geometric designs, seen from all viewpoints and with sectional views, to presentation drawings with all details in 1:1 scale.

Materials   Prepared wood is mostly used for frames and box constructions, whereas manufactured board, e.g. plywood, is used for slab constructions.

Furniture carcases   These not only have to be well-joined, but also have to be given rigidity, e.g. by a back panel, so that the doors shut properly.

Assembly   Furniture can be assembled in various ways and using various approaches, depending on the joints used and whether or not it is to be dismantled at a later date.

Joints   Rectangular joints are easiest to make, but angled or rounded joints are also possible.

Fittings   Various types of fittings offer a number of ways of opening doors, flaps and drawers, as well as keeping them closed with knobs, catches, bolts or locks.

Frames   Chair, beds and table frames are subject to great stress and must therefore be particularly well-made.

Planning and graphics

Planning

The **draft** should combine material, colour and texture to create a functional structure. This sets the standard for the quality of the finished article. Depending on the type of craft chosen, whether joinery, woodturning, carving, intarsia or moulding, furniture may appear hard or soft, light or heavy, plain or elaborate.

The draft should also include any thoughts about the use and construction of the object. When considering the use of a piece of furniture, think about the differences between cupboards, chairs, tables, shelves and built-in furniture.

The **constructional design** is mainly concerned with the joints to be used, the rigidity of the object, its statics, stability and durability. Construction and function are closely connected to each other, and these determine whether a piece of furniture is to be a permanent structure or if it can be taken apart.

There is a whole assortment of joining systems available today that enable relatively quick and simple assembly. However, the range of traditional woodworking methods such as using tenons, pins and rebate joints is still useful, and some techniques are being rediscovered.

Design

Unlike free art forms, furniture design is directly connected to function. The use of naturally grown wood, with such specific properties as structure, elasticity, changes in shape etc., imposes certain restrictions on the woodworker. Your design should suit modern needs and tastes and express the spirit of the time. You should therefore avoid the wholesale imitation of past styles as much as possible.

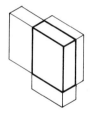

Planning

Plans for furniture should include design, form and colouring, function (e.g. writing desk with lid), a structure suiting the material used, quality of workmanship, a list of materials and costing calculations. Before any concrete plans can be made, the idea should be conceived and sketches made. From these develop a draft which is then drawn more precisely. The desired quality of craftmanship, available tools and available time must also be considered.

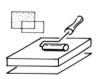

Surface treatment

This serves to improve the object visually as well as to protect it against the elements. There are two main alternatives:
1 The wood is seen to be wood: by staining, dying, varnishing, matt finishing, polishing or waxing. A good quality wood is essential for this.
2 The wood is not seen to be wood: by painting, or covering with adhesive plastic sheeting or synthetic materials. Manufactured boards or lower quality wood may be used here.

Graphics

Drawing is used to develop, clarify and establish all the details of the design and construction.
First draw up a rough, preliminary sketch of the piece of furniture. When your ideas have been developed, make a further sketch to show construction details. A working drawing showing all the views, sections, details, measurements of the piece of furniture and the materials list can then be drawn to scale. Finally a cutting list can be added. A perspective or isometric drawing is useful in forming a realistic impression of the finished piece.

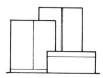

Types of furniture

There are many distinct types of furniture, e.g. box or stool-frame constructions.

All cupboards, wardrobes and chests are box constructions. Stool-frame constructions are used mainly for chairs and tables – these in particular are subject to great stress and because of this they are usually made of solid wood.

Another distinction should be made between permanent furniture and that which can be taken apart and reassembled. Cupboards and beds often fall into this category. Chairs and tables are usually permanent, i.e. they cannot be taken apart, and at the most may be folded for storage etc. Shelves can be either free-standing or wall-mounted.

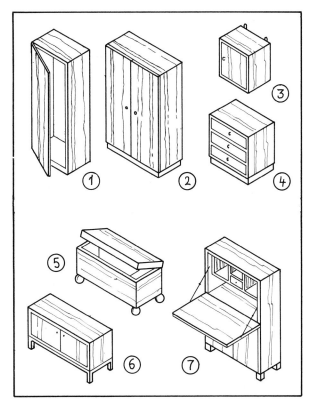

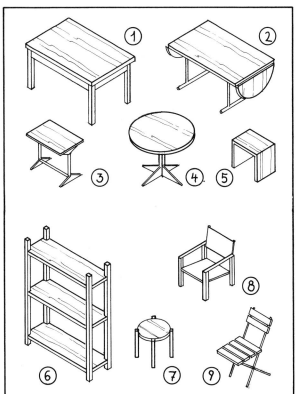

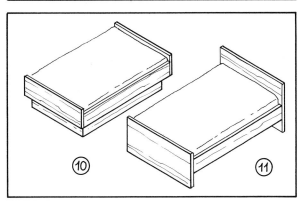

Box constructions
1 cupboard with one door
2 cupboard with two doors
3 wall-mounted cupboard
4 chest-of-drawers
5 chest
6 sideboard
7 bureau

Stool-frame constructions
1 table
2 drop leaf table
3 side table
4 round dining table
5 coffee table
6 shelves
7 stool
8 arm chair
9 chair

Beds
10 on a pedestal, the side rails carrying the head and foot boards
11 the head and foot boards carrying the side rails

11

Construction plans

These include plans for assembling the furniture (according to the materials used, the function, the design and the method of production) as well as keeping within any specified costing.

After these have been drawn up the details of the construction can be decided on.

There are two distinct categories:

1 Box constructions, consisting of glued, solid timber boards or manufactured boards, e.g. chipboard or blockboard.

2 Frame constructions, consisting of solid wooden frames inset with panels made of solid wood, plywood or glass.

The order in which the various parts of a piece of furniture are assembled is just as important, e.g. first the main body along with fixed inside walls or shelves, then the back and finally the doors.

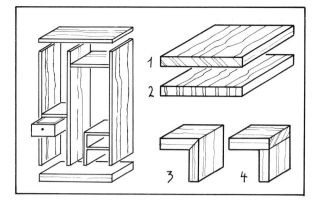

Planning construction
● assembly, e.g.:
  order of assembly
  elements (e.g. drawers)
  function
● choice of material, e.g.:
  1 solid wood
  2 manufactured board
● construction, e.g.:
  stool-frame construction
  box construction
● details, e.g.:
  3 mitred joint
  4 butt joint

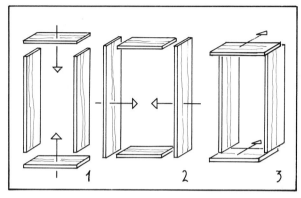

Assembly type
● permanent or 'knockdown' (i.e. can be reassembled)
● order of assembly, e.g.:
  1 top and bottom on sides
  2 sides against top and bottom
  3 top and bottom pushed onto sides

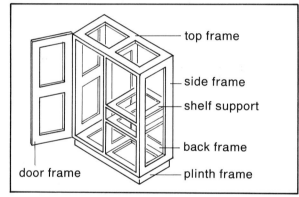

Example of frame construction
This frame construction follows a traditional method of construction well suited to wood. Here frames and panels provide a base for fixed or movable parts.

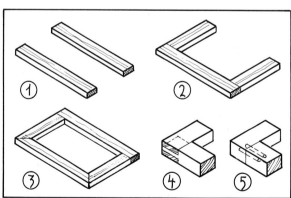

Frame elements
1 part of frame
  e.g. carcase joints
2 open frame
  e.g. drawer runners
3 closed frame
  e.g. rim, plinth, side, door

Frame joints
4 tongue and groove
5 dowel

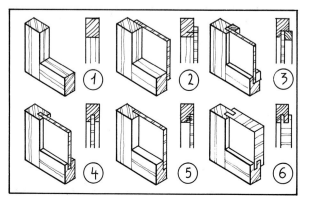

Frames and panels
1 frame, open, no panel
2 panel nailed on
3 in rebate, with beading
4 held in groove
5 glued into rebate
6 overlapping frame

Construction plans

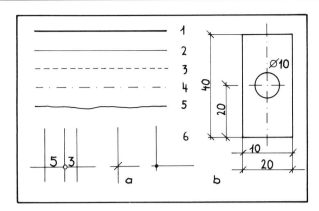

Basic terms
1 continuous line, bold:
   visible edges and outlines
2 continuous line, medium:
   hatching, dimension lines
3 dotted line:
   hidden detail lines, contours
4 dot-dash line:
   centre lines, cutting planes
5 freehand lines:
   hatching, breakage line
6 dimension limit lines

Cutting planes
1 solid wood (cross cut)
2 blockboard, 16mm ($\frac{5}{8}$in)
3 veneered board
4 laminated board, 19mm ($\frac{3}{4}$in)
   maple veneer
   X = cross cut
5 solid wood (grain wood)
6 chipboard
7 hardboard
8a stone on wood
8b steel plate

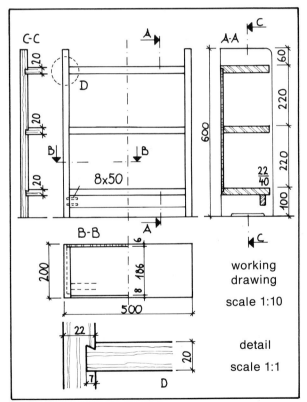

working
drawing

scale 1:10

detail

scale 1:1

Working drawing
Scales
1:20, 1:10, 1:5
Details: 1:1
When making furniture the
following views are necessary:
front elevation, top view (plan),
side elevation, cross-sections

Cross-sections give a better
view of internal construction
details.

Differentiate between:
● cross-sectional plan B-B,
   parallel to ground
● cross-sectional front elevation
   C-C, parallel to front view
● cross-sectional side elevation
   A-A, 90° to front view

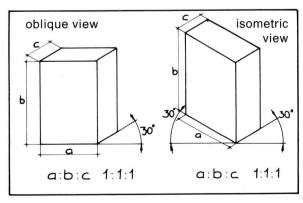

Three-dimensional views
(no foreshortening)
● Oblique view: side to front,
   side and top views at 30° to
   front
● Isometric view: corner to front,
   30°

Cupboards

Parts

Cupboard design is always
influenced by the intended use
i.e. as a place to store particular
objects in, and therefore you
should always take into account
the room it is in.
Cupboards may stand against a
wall, in a corner or remain free
standing. Their size sometimes
depends on the transport
available, though many
commercially-produced
cupboards are designed to be
easily transported and
assembled.

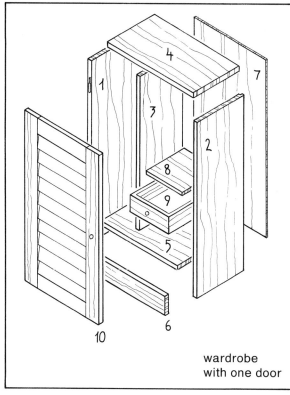

wardrobe
with one door

Cupboard parts
1 hinge
2 side panel
3 centre panel
4 top panel
5 bottom panel
6 plinth front
7 back board (for rigidity and
    to keep off dust)
8 shelf
9 drawer
10 door (e.g. with louvre panels)

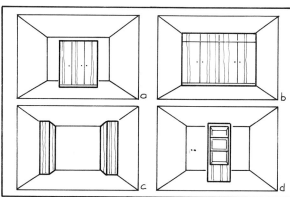

Cupboard placement
Cupboard types
a) against a wall, as an
    individual piece of furniture
b) as a wall unit, built-in
c) to emphasize the space
    vertically
d) as a room divider,
    free-standing

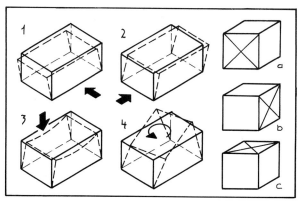

Rigidity is necessary to prevent
the furniture from:
1/2 moving sideways
3   sagging
4   warping
Rigidity can be provided by:
Panels, boards, wire, cleats,
diagonally across all planes,
singly or crossed (a–c)

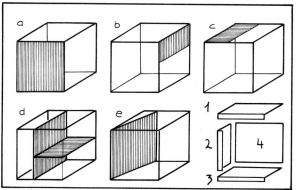

Constructions become more
stable with panels which cover a
whole surface (a) rather than just
part of one (b) and (c). Horizontal,
vertical (d) or diagonal (e) inner
panels also provide a very high
level of rigidity.

Stabilizing elements:
1 cornice
2 pilaster strip
3 plinth
4 back panel

Construction methods

Wall units can be assembled in various ways by combining smaller elements to form the whole, e.g. cabinet sections. Units can range from the simplest combinations to purpose-built units in set measurements.

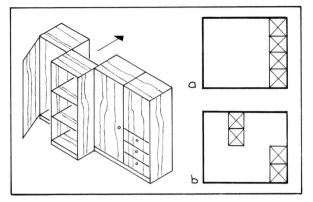

Cupboard units
By combining units with the same measurements
a) wall units and
b) room dividers can be created.

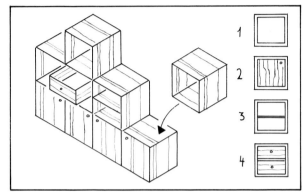

Single cabinets in a standard size, e.g. cubes, provide a variety of possible combinations. Each cabinet is stable and they can be stacked.

Variations:
1 open cabinet
2 cabinet with door
3 cabinet with shelf
4 cabinet with drawers

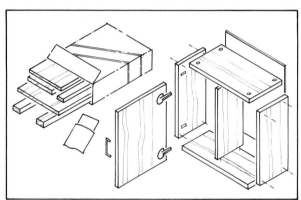

Pre-packed furniture which is transported by the buyer is usually for self assembly and has special 'knockdown' fittings for easy assembly.

Advantages:
easy transport in cartons, easy self assembly without special tools, and good value for money.

Disadvantages:
workmanship and fit not always satisfactory.

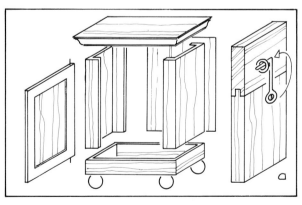

Traditional cupboards can also often be dismantled. The fastenings are usually at the sides or by the plinth or cornice. Hooks and eyes or wedges are used here.

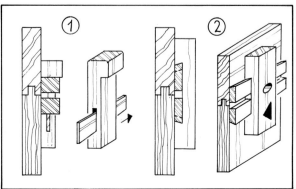

Traditional cupboard fastenings
1 key fastenings: a wooden key with a head at one end is pushed through the frame of the plinth or the cornice and the beading.
2 the fastening, made with a conical groove, is pushed along two tapered ledges with matching edges.

Knockdown fittings

Cupboards which can be dismantled are easy to transport and can easily be packed in cartons; and a variety of ingenious joints assures quick assembly. The rigidity of these structures is somewhat limited, however. The simplest joint is made with a screw, while more complicated joints are concealed and comprise several parts which are fastened by turning.

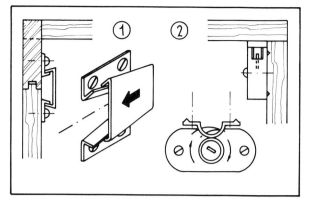

Wedged joints
1 fixed by wedging a tapered cap (using a hammer)
2 fixed by turning a conical clamp wheel (using a screwdriver). This type of joint is often found on older furniture.

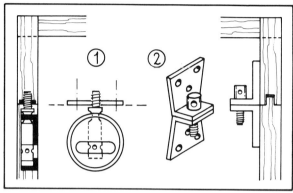

Traditional screw joints
1 traditional screw joint, recessed into sides and cornice, fastened with a bradawl; note that the recessing requires skill.
2 traditional screw joint, screwed onto sides and cornice, fastened with a bradawl; very easy to mount, but projects into the cupboard interior.

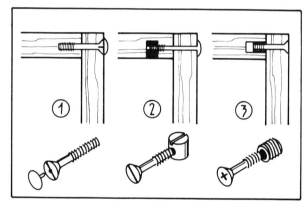

Screw joints
1 single screw and cup
2 fine threaded screw and plastic cross dowel
3 countersunk head screw with Philips head and brass bolt
All three types are visible.

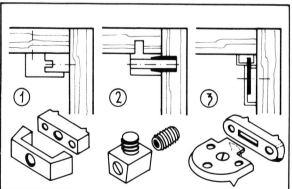

Block fittings
1 corner jointing block
2 chipboard insert
3 eccentric block
All three types project into the cupboard interior.

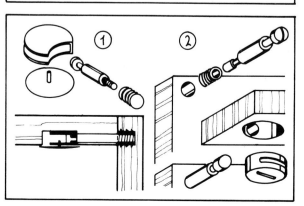

Cam fitting
Order of assembly:
using a jig bore holes and a cylinder. Drive in the fix cam and screw in the joint bolt. Assemble the carcase parts, put the eccentric fitting into the cylinder and fasten the cam with a screwdriver.

Advantages:
concealed from outside, covered from inside.

Permanent joints

Joints are generally permanent or non-permanent, i.e. they may be taken apart. This section focuses on permanent wood joints. The type of joint used depends on the material chosen, while the structure and construction of corner joints also depend on the design, e.g. straight or rounded corners.

Corner joints also have an additional structural function, e.g. a cupboard foot has to absorb the weight of the plinth, or, at the back of a cupboard, it has to support the back panel (rigidity).

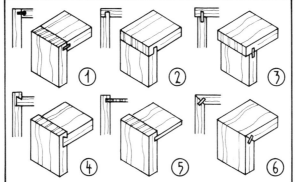

Cupboard corners, top
Depending on the design, there are various ways of constructing cupboard corners:
1   side continues
2   top continues
3   top overlaps
4/5 sides project
6   flush, mitred

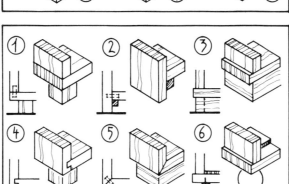

Cupboard corners, bottom (plinth)
1 side on bottom
2 side continues
3 continuous plinth
4 on single foot
5 mitre joint (plinth)
6 on ball foot

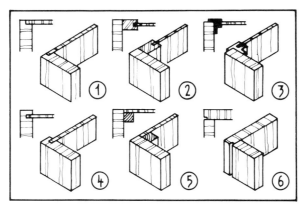

Back panels serve both as the back wall of the cupboard and to give it rigidity.

Joints:
1 rebate
2 butt
3 plastic clamp
4 housing
5 with square section block
6 strengthened back, butt joint, with decorative groove

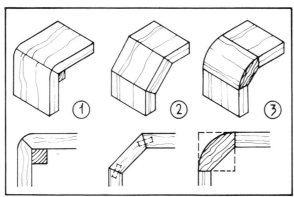

Edging, horizontal
1 rounded, two-part, with square section block
2 angular, three-part
3 round, three-part, central piece from square block

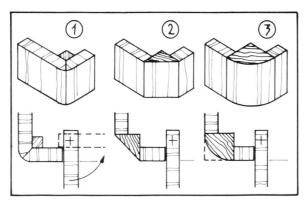

Edging, vertical
1 rounded, two-part, with square section block
2 angular, three-part
3 round, three-part, central piece rounded from square block
The sections show hinged doors.

17

Doors

Hinged doors

There are various types of hinged doors and different ways of fitting them. Doors tend to be either flat frame constructions with panels or slab constructions from manufactured boards.

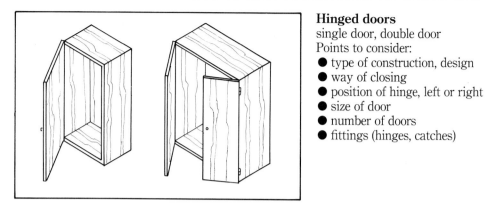

Hinged doors
single door, double door
Points to consider:
- type of construction, design
- way of closing
- position of hinge, left or right
- size of door
- number of doors
- fittings (hinges, catches)

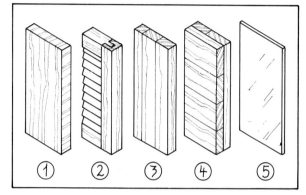

Type of door
1 slab, simple block or chipboard
2 flat frame construction with louvre panel, e.g. linen cupboard
3 slab of solid wood planking
4 slab, double layer of wood glued at right angles
5 glass door

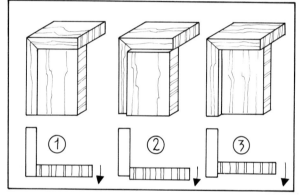

Methods of fitting
1 inside frame, flush to front, exact fit required
2 projecting forwards, with a large choice of hinges possible
3 inside frame
4 sunk into cupboard frame, dustproof, elaborate construction
5 front fitting, simple construction as door does not have to fit flush
6 rebate fitting, dustproof

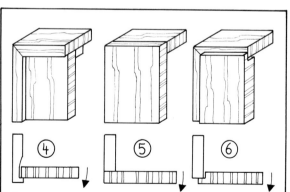

Central openings
only possible with double doors
1 open
2 with stile, inside
3 with stile, outside
4 overlap
5 overlap, wide groove
6 rounded overlap

Sliding doors

Unlike hinged doors, sliding doors are not in the way when open, but they always conceal half of the cupboard interior, e.g. with two doors on parallel tracks. Note the difference between sliding and gliding doors. The whole lower surface of a sliding door usually runs along a rail or in a groove. Gliding doors run along tracks on rollers and are easier to move. Both types of door can be set in place or removed by lifting and moving at an angle, and they can also be locked. Suspended sliding doors should have a lower guide rail to prevent swinging.

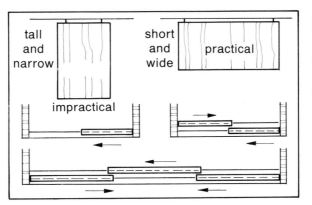

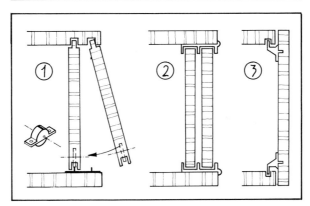

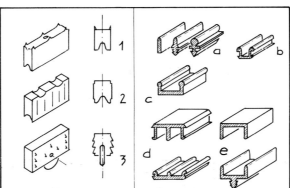

Sizes
tall: rollers are necessary to prevent tilting (gliding doors)
short: can easily be moved along tracks without rollers (sliding doors)
dual doors: when both cupboards are to be closed at least two tracks are required.

Construction
1 running between top and base
2 running below top and against base
3 running against top and base

Sunken handles enable doors on different tracks to slide past each other.

Arrangements
1 inside wide groove
2 top inside groove, bottom on rail
3/4 on top and base rails (smooth running)
5 suspended, with angular fittings in grooves

Details
1 on rollers, easily removable
2 in plastic channels, sliding
3 special form where a suspended sliding door moves along using plastic runners in grooves

Fittings for gliding doors
1/2 plastic gliding tracks
3 plastic roller, usually recessed into door

Tracks
a) single track
b) for glass doors
c) two channels, for rollers
d) two channels, for gliding tracks
e) two channels, for gliding tracks at top or bottom of grooved door

Hinges

Hinges are the movable element that join doors, flaps or lids to cupboards. Some doors can be lifted out of their hinges, while some hinges allow the fitting of the door to be adjusted after fixing (usually necessary with front-fitting doors).

Continuous hinges (piano hinges) are simple to fit. When fitting hinges that can be lifted apart it is important to distinguish between right- and left-fitting doors. Hinges are made from steel and nickel, then brass- or chrome-plated, polished or varnished. Some modern recessed hinges are made partly of plastic.

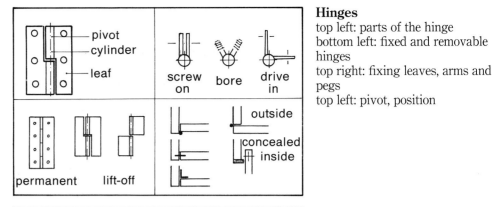

Hinges
top left: parts of the hinge
bottom left: fixed and removable hinges
top right: fixing leaves, arms and pegs
top left: pivot, position

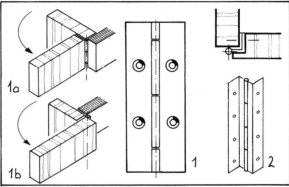

Piano hinges are available in lengths of up to 3.5m (11½ ft). They are easy to fix, versatile and good value for money; however, the screws do tend to become loose after long use.
1 a) and b) simple piano hinge
2 angular hinge (for rebated doors)

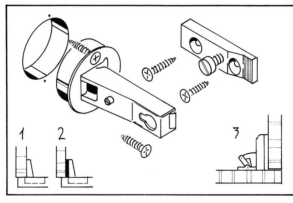

Sprung, concealed hinges consist of the pivot, arm and mounting plate, and are only suitable for front-fitting doors. They stay open at the position desired, are relatively easy to fit and available in various forms and types.
1/2 use of mounting plate to adjust door position
3 180° hinge

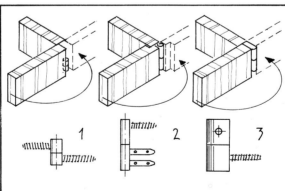

Bored hinges are suitable for doors opening to the left or right. The hinges are screwed or driven in. Very easy assembly, low price, and the option of lifting the door out of the hinges make these very attractive.
1 short hinge
2 long hinge
3 half-rounded hinge, only for front-fitting doors

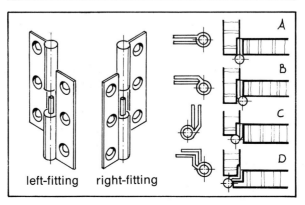

Lift-off hinges
These look similar to butt hinges, but have the advantage that they can be lifted apart. They are used for high-quality furniture and, depending on the angle, they can be used for front-fitting, receding and rebated doors.
A: straight version
B/C: cranked
D: angular

The choice of hinge depends on the quality of the furniture desired and the degree of skilled workmanship available. Pivot-type hinges are costly, but are completely hidden. The angle of the door opening must be taken into account, e.g. 90° or 180°, as well as whether it opens to the left or right, etc.

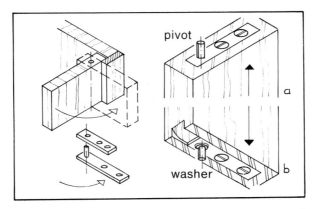

Centric pivot-type hinges are recessed and concealed in the top and bottom of the door. Opening angle: 90°
The door is checked by a pilaster strip or a bolt in the base.
a) from above
b) from below

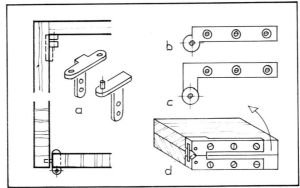

Eccentric pivot-type hinges are recessed in the top and bottom of the door, but are still visible.
a) opening: almost 180°
b) cranked pivot hinge
c) angular pivot hinge
d) card table hinge

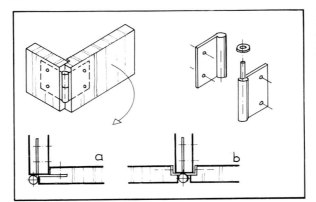

Pivot hinges
For rebated doors. The leaf is fitted into a mortized slot and held in position from outside by pins. Fitting requires great skill. Opening; 180°. The door can be lifted off its hinges.
a) simple pivot hinge
b) cranked pivot hinge, for two doors simultaneously

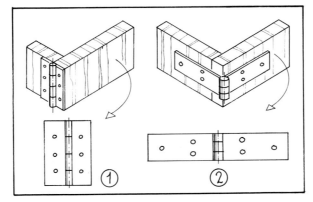

Butt hinges for simple furniture and easy, visible asembly.
Opening: 180°
It is not possible to lift the door off its hinges.
1 narrow to medium-wide
2 square to wide

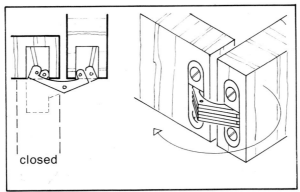

Vicci hinges
recessed and concealed in door and carcase sides
Opening: 180°
Relatively easy to assemble, they close gently and are versatile.

Roll tops, flaps and lids

Roll tops

Roll tops can be pushed entirely to the side, top or bottom, so that cupboards can be opened right out. However, they do need considerable space. The radius of the bend must not be too small.

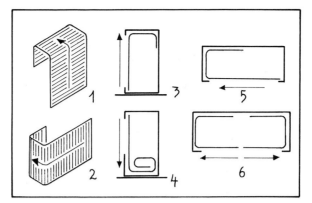

Direction of roll top
1 vertical
2 horizontal
3 upwards
4 downwards
5 to one side
6 to two sides

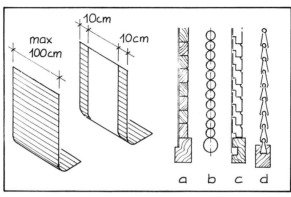

Roll top battens
Material: hardwood, plastic
Measurements: 1000mm (39in) maximum
Attachments; canvas, bands, straps, string
a) flat battens, fastened to straps
b) bored round battens, joined by string
c) caterpillar profile, dustproof
d) plastic, pieces clipped together

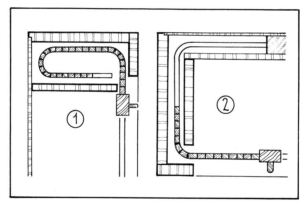

Ways of fitting roll tops
1 vertical, e.g. rolled up in top of cupboard
2 horizontal, e.g. behind false back
Note: the larger the radius, the easier to move the roll top.

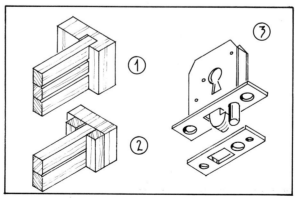

Tracks
1 mortized groove in carcase side
2 strips of wood glued onto sides; curves are difficult, however.
Note: The groove must be 1mm wider than the battens to avoid friction.
3 tambour or sliding door lock

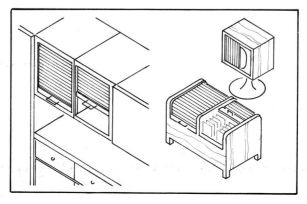

Uses
office furniture
wall-mounted cupboards
filing cabinets
TV cabinets

Flaps and lids

Flaps are similar to doors, except that they open horizontally and need to withstand the strain of being used as writing desks, or the weight of objects placed on them. They are commonly found on bureaux as well as on chests. There are various ways of supporting the flaps and keeping them in a horizontal position. A drop-leaf table can save space in a small room and is made by fixing a flap to the wall. Larger drop-leaf tables can also be made, usually in two parts, one of which forms a support.

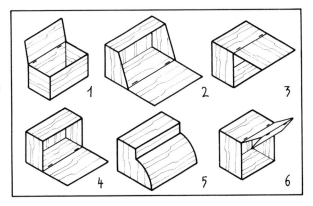

Types of flap
1 lid, e.g. chest lid
2 oblique, e.g. writing desk
3 lift-up flap, support necessary
4 drop-down, support necessary
5 rounded, bonnet in one piece or as roll top
6 lift-up, split flap, e.g. wall-mounted kitchen cupboard

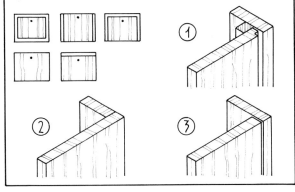

Writing desk
Positions:
1 free-standing
2 against wall
3 wall-mounted
4 built-in
a) alternative methods of use

Number of hinges:
Over 900mm (35in) width three single hinges required

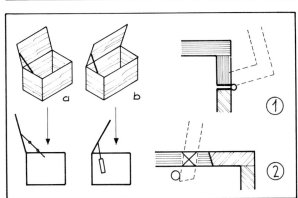

Ways of closing flaps
Depending on the design:
1 flap closes inside, against screwed block of wood
2 flap closes outside
3 flap closes inside, simple version

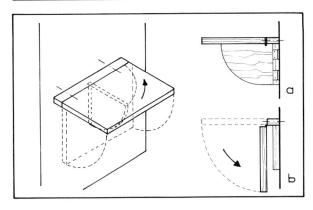

Chest lids
Opening angles:
a) with stays or chain > 90°
b) with lid support < 90°, here used as a brake

Position of fitting:
1 on the back
2 in the lid

Wall flaps
(drop-leaf table). Used in small kitchens as breakfast table etc, and relatively simple assembly.
a) assembled, with swing-out bracket
b) folded when not in use

Flap fittings

Supports and stays keep the flap in a horizontal position. The simplest support is a post standing below the flap, though sliding brackets are more elegant. There are various types of stays from the simple to the pneumatic which enable the flap to glide open gently.

Flap hinges form the movable joint between a flap and a cupboard. They are usually recessed and screwed into position. Particularly useful hinges are those that allow a flush joint between flap and cupboard.

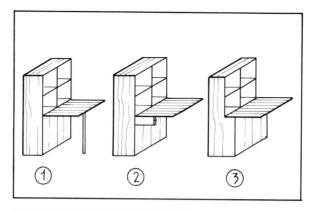

Supports
1 with leg attachment, folding
2 with sliding brackets
3 supported by cupboard itself, either partially or right across

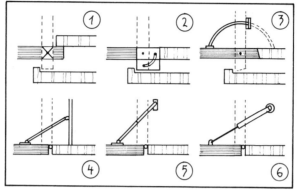

Stays
1 flap checked under shelf
2 with special hinge
3 with bow-shaped metal stay
4 gliding stay
5 scissor-type stay
6 pneumatic stay

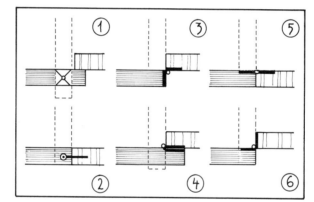

Position of hinges
● in the flap
  1 butt hinge
  2 butt hinge, flush joint
● below the flap
  3 continuous hinge
  4 butt hinge
  5 flap hinge, flush joint
  6 continuous hinge, hinge inside

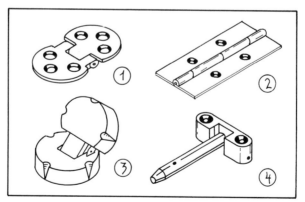

Hinges
1 flap hinge
2 butt hinge, easy assembly
3 recessed flap hinge
4 bore hinge

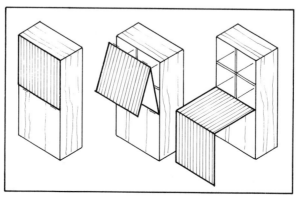

Folding table consisting of two parts: one drop leaf as table top and one as the side support. Practical, but heavy and costly to make.

Locks and catches

Locks

There are different types of locks. Depending on the door to be fitted, left- or right-hand locks are used.

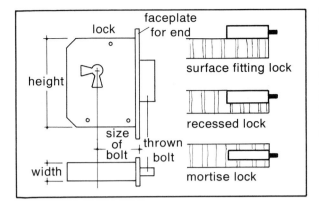

Depending on the thickness of the door, locks may be screwed onto the surface, recessed or mortized. The size of the bolt determines the dimensions of the lock.
Locks are available with double keyholes for use in box constructions.

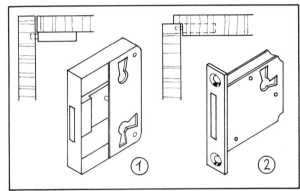

Locks for box constructions
1 for simple furniture, fitted to the inside of the door; easily assembled with screws

Mortise locks
2 for double doors or rebated doors, mortized into the door. The mortise has to be bored and chiselled out.

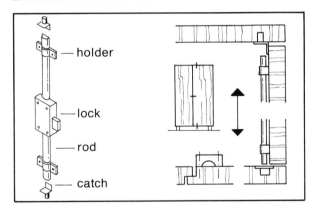

Wardrobe locks
For tall doors and tall double doors. The key turning moves the rods up and/or down behind the catches.

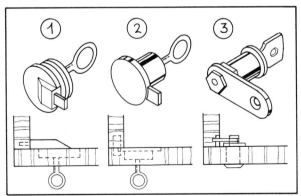

Cylindrical recessed locks for all types of doors
1 with bolt, surface fitting
2 with bolt, concealed
3 with catch and safety cylinder

Fitting:
a hole for the lock is bored, the lock is fitted in and secured with screws.

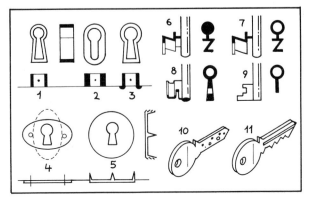

Keys and keyholes
1–3 keyhole fittings, recessed
4/5 keyplates, surface-fitting

Key wards
6 closed
7–9 bored
10/11 for rim locks

Catches

Catches can be used instead of
locks to keep doors closed. They
are usually fitted on the inside of
doors which they keep closed
mechanically or with magnets.
There are various ways of fixing
catches, depending on how easily
the door is to be opened.
Bolts are only used on double
doors, i.e. one door can only be
opened from the inside when the
other door, which is fitted with a
lock, is already open. Surface
fitting or recessed catches are
available, usually made of metal
or plastic.

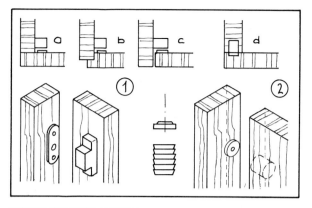

Magnetic catches can be used
for closing doors in all ways
(a–c). Cylindrical catches are
inserted into a bored hole (d).
1 magnetic catch on carcase,
   striking plate on door
2 cylindrical catch in carcase,
   striking plate on door

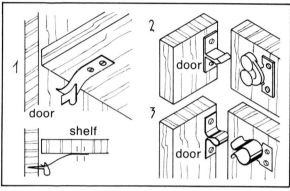

Spring catches only used on
cupboards with double doors.
1 door with hook bolt, shelf with
   steel spring. When the door is
   closed the steel spring snaps
   into the hook bolt.
2 double roller catch, plastic
3 gripper catch, metal

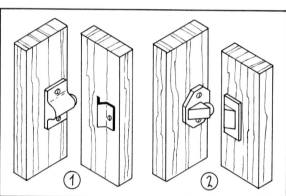

Ball catches
1 metal
2 plastic
Useful for small furniture and
doors etc, closing all ways; easily
fitted by screwing.

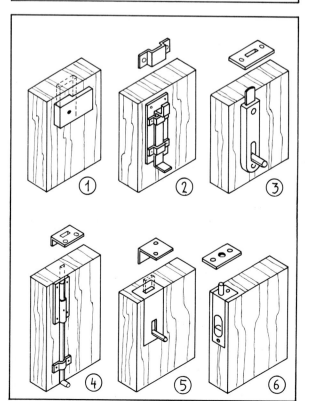

Bolts only used with double
doors, e.g. wardrobes
1   wooden bolt, closed position
     when turned upwards
2   bolt, cranked, for doors
     which project forwards
3   bolt, straight, with locking
     plate
4   wardrobe bolt, for tall doors
5/6 recessed bolts.

Advantage: added cupboard
space.
Disadvantage: complicated to fit.

Knobs and handles

Knobs and handles are used to open and close drawers, flaps, roll tops and doors. Therefore they should be constructed with this in mind, i.e. without sharp edges or too small to grip easily. Neither should they stick out too far; to avoid causing injury.
As well as knobs and handles, projecting or recessed rails, usually running along the whole width of a drawer, can also be used. A great variety of different materials can be employed, enhancing the design of the piece.

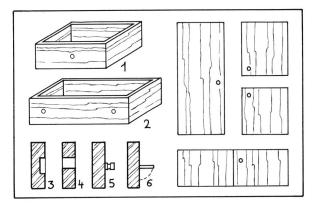

Arrangements
1 on drawers, e.g. centrally on narrow drawers, double knobs on wide drawers
2 on doors, e.g. tall doors, square and double doors

Types
3 recessed (pull)
4 open (hole)
5 projecting (knob)
6 falling (drop)

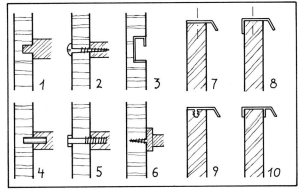

Fittings
1   pin, screwed
2   screwed from inside
3   plastic rail, recessed
4   dowelled
5   screwed
6   screw in knob
7–10 plastic or metal profile along whole width as rail; screwed, glued, grooved or wedged

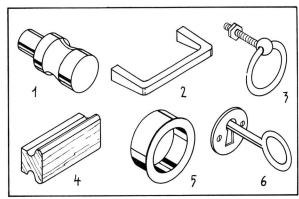

Individual handles for drawers and doors
1 wooden knob
2 squared handle
3 ring pull
4 moulded rail
5 recessed pull
6 lock, key serves as handle

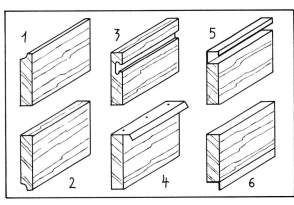

Continuous rails usually used on drawers
1–3 top or bottom edge, invisible; or as a groove
4–6 metal or plastic, screwed onto top or bottom edge

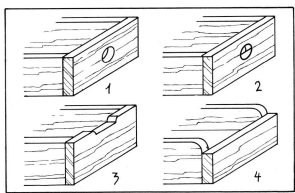

Special forms usually for bureaux or wardrobes
1 simple hole
2 pull, glued
3 cut away handle
4 inset drawer (wardrobes)
Note: These special forms are only dustproof up to a point!

Drawers

Fitting Drawers

There are different ways of fitting drawers: some move along runners and some on side rails from which they are suspended. Drawers made of solid wood are usually joined by dovetail joints. Drawers may be visible or concealed behind doors.

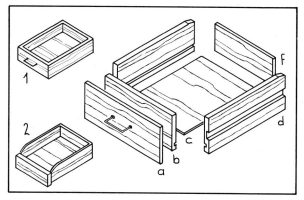

Drawers
1 at front of furniture, visible
2 inset drawer, front only half height, concealed behind doors, e.g. in wardrobe.

Parts
a) false front
b) true front
c) drawer bottom
d) drawer side
e) drawer back

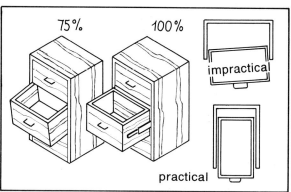

Conventional drawers can be pulled out to three-quarters of their depth – using telescope rails they can be pulled out completely. Wide drawers tilt and jam easily; deep, narrow drawers are better.

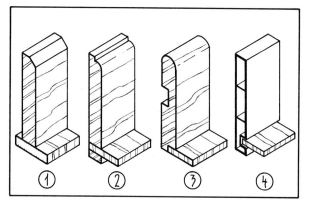

Sides and bottoms
1 side bevelled at top; solid bottom with overlap
2 side rabbeted at top; bottom made of plywood with lower runner
3 side rounded at top, side grooved (suspended drawer); bottom fitted into rebate
4 side of moulded plastic, bottom set into groove

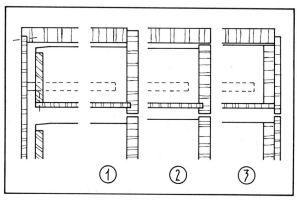

Ways of closing
1 drawer fits outside carcase; this also acts as a stop
2 drawer fits inside carcase; carcase and rail visible
3 rabbeted drawer; false front; dustproof

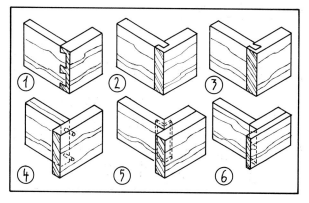

Corner joints
1 lap dovetail, concealed (very strong joint)
2 tongued joint
3 dovetail (very strong)
4 dowelled joint
5 mitred joint with right angled tongue
6 through dovetail, false front necessary

Drawers on runners

Drawers with runners at the bottom are good for frequent use, as the weight of the drawer falls mainly on the runners. The sides and the frame should be made of solid hardwood, as these parts wear with use. Bevelled edges at the back of drawers enable easier fitting into carcases. The bottoms are made of plywood or hardboard panels.

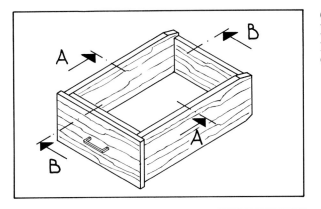

Construction

Drawer on runners, isometric projection showing the views discussed below

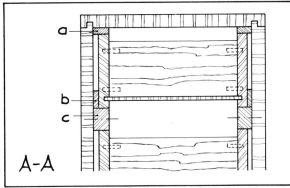

Front section A-A

a) kicker
b) guide, serves to keep side of drawer in position
c) runner, also kicker for drawer below

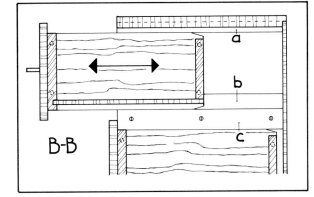

Vertical section B-B

a) to c) see front section A-A. False front serves as stop. The back edges of the drawer have been bevelled, enabling the drawer to be fitted into the furniture carcase more easily and preventing tilting.

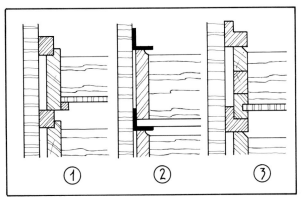

Special constructions

1 Wooden runner with rebated drawer side
2 L-shaped metal profile, space-saving rails, simple assembly
3 Rebated wooden rail

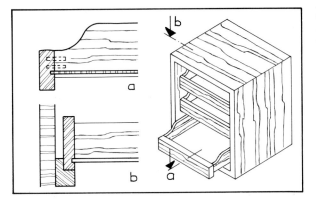

Inset drawers are found in separate drawer elements in wardrobes or desks. The half-open front serves as a handle and gives a view of the drawer contents.

Side-hung drawers

Side-hung drawers are fitted with the grooves in the sides serving as runner, side rail and kicker. The maximum depth of the groove in the sides should be one-third of the side, to ensure sufficient stability. Telescope rails are an exception: these are screwed to the sides of the drawers and attached by rollers to the guide rails, which are in turn attached to the carcase. Detachable telescope rails are also available.

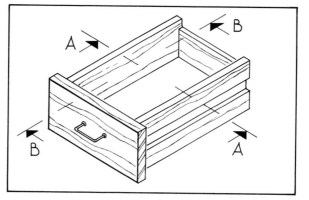

Construction
Side-hung drawer
Isometric projection showing the views discussed below.

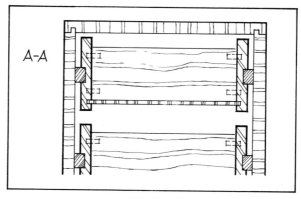

Front section A-A
The maximum depth of the groove should be one-third of the width of the side. The runner also serves as kicker and side rail. The rails are screwed onto the carcase. Bevelled edges create less friction.

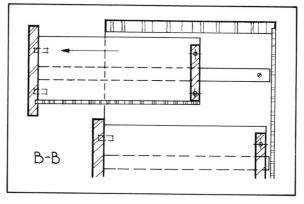

Vertical section B-B
Side-hung drawer closes outside carcase.
Note: Drawers glide better if the rails have been rubbed with soap! Synthetic rails can also ensure easy gliding.

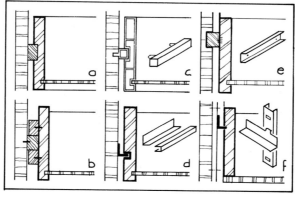

Rails
a) wood
b) wood, with two side rails
c) prefabricated synthetic rails
d) metal rails
e) glued wooden side rail in U-shaped moulded plastic
f) removable metal rail, adjustable vertically, e.g. in shelving

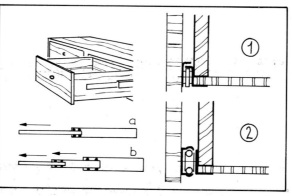

Telescopic rails greatly increase the degree to which drawers can be opened and are smooth running. They consist of a special profile with:
1 rollers or
2 ball bearings.
The telescope may consist of one a), or more b), extensions.

Shelves and stool-frame constructions

Free-standing shelves

The main difference between wall-mounted and free-standing shelves is that the latter consist either of solid wooden frames or slab constructions with side panels. They are given rigidity either by firmly fitted shelves or by additional stabilizing elements.

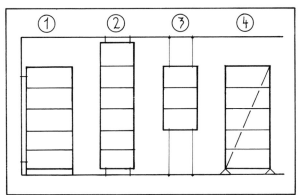

Types
1 connected to wall, stable construction
2 connected to ceiling and floor, room high, very stable
3 hanging, e.g. on rope or wire
4 free-standing, with diagonal battens to aid stability

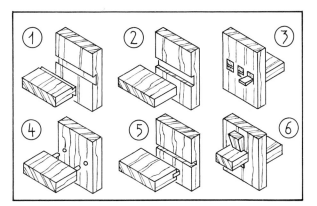

Rigidity is aided by:
a) fitted shelves
b) back panels
c) diagonals; rope, wire or cleats
d) corners strengthened by triangular blocks

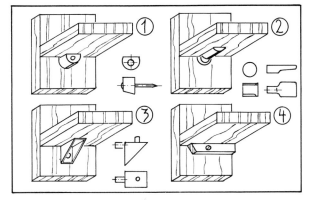

Corner joints
1, 3, 6 are recommended for solid wood
2, 4, 5 are recommended for manufactured board

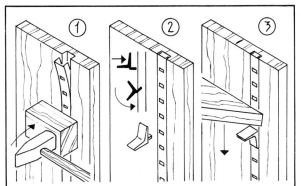

Shelf supports
1 plastic support, nailed
2 metal dowel in casing
3 triangular plastic support with pin for shelf
4 cleat, screwed

Rails made of metal or plastic can be used, allowing the height of the shelves to be adjustable. For example:
1 set the rail in its groove
2 fix the supports
3 fit the shelf, holding it at an angle

Wall-mounted shelves

Wall-mounted shelves usually consist of metal rails screwed vertically to the wall, brackets which are fitted into the holes or slots in the rails, and the shelves themselves.

Reasonably priced, expandable shelving systems are available from retailers.

The metal parts are painted. The height of the shelves, made of solid wood or manufactured board, is adjustable. They are either hung in a metal frame or held by brackets.

Joining two shelves at the same level may require double brackets or wider supports. Books can be held by added book ends.

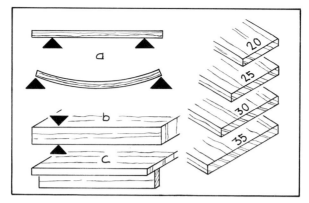

Shelf dimensions depend on the material used, the support, the expected load and use of the shelf. To prevent sagging:
a) maximum distance between brackets 800mm (31in) for 19mm shelves
b) thicker board, e.g. 32mm ($1\frac{1}{4}$in)
c) reinforcement strip, screwed from below
Recommended depth for shelves: 200–350mm ($\frac{7}{8}$–$1\frac{3}{16}$in)

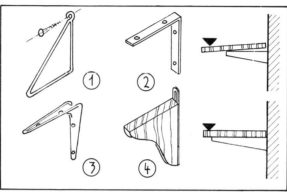

Frames and brackets
1 wire frame
2 metal bracket
3 reinforced metal bracket
4 wooden bracket
Note: The size of the frames and brackets should not be less than $\frac{3}{4}$ the depth of the shelves!

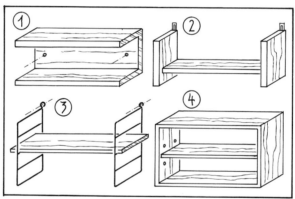

Single shelves
1 with fixed back panel
2 with side panels (book ends)
3 metal frame
4 carcase with adjustable shelf

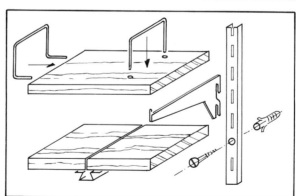

Shelving systems consisting of wall-mounted, U-profiled rails of different lengths, with slots for brackets.
These expandable systems are available from retailers.

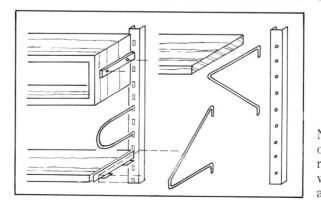

Not only shelves, but cupboards, open or with doors, magazine racks, upright book ends and wire frames or brackets are also available.

Stool-frame constructions

This type of framework is found on tables, chairs, beds and as the base of cupboards. Its function is to support and such frames are usually made of solid wood. Since loads have to be supported, the joints, frames, sections and stabilizing elements have to be well thought out. With the exception of bedsteads, most stool-frame constructions cannot be taken apart.

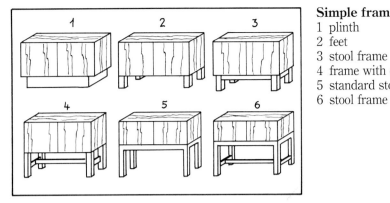

Simple frames
1 plinth
2 feet
3 stool frame
4 frame with central truss
5 standard stool frame
6 stool frame with central truss

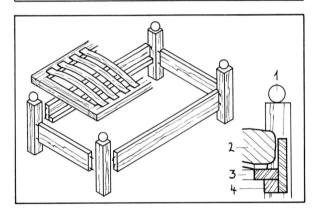

Special frames
1 chair
2 table
3 U-shaped side frame
4 square side frame
5 runner
6 posts

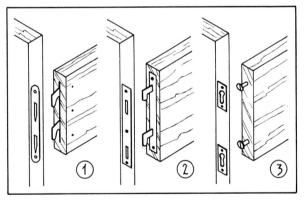

Bedsteads can usually be taken apart; they consist of side rails, headboard and footboard, and metal or wooden slatted frames
1 bedpost
2 mattress
3 frame
4 side rail with block to support frame

Bedstead fittings – attach the side rails to the bedstocks
1 slot fitting
2 traditional fitting
3 round head screw fitting

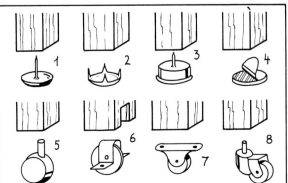

Glides and castors for movable furniture, e.g. chairs
1 buffer
2 glide
3 rubber buffer
4 felt buffer
5 ball castor with ferrule fitting
6 castor, fitted into mortise
7 castor, plate screwed from below
8 castor, can be swivelled

Tables and chairs

Tables

Tables generally consist of a frame (legs and rails) and a top. Stretchers give the frame rigidity. A central pedestal is popular for round or square tables. Dining table tops are generally 1300 × 800mm (51 × 31in). The height of the table top, and also of desk tops, is about 740mm (29in), the knee height over 620mm (24in)

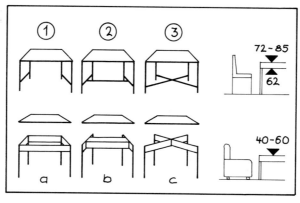

Stretchers
1 side
2 side, with central truss
3 diagonal

Rails
a) four sides
b) side and centre
c) diagonal

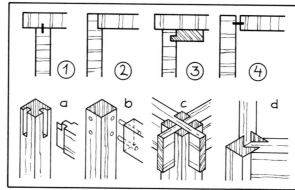

Table tops
1 dowelled to rail
2 recessed into rail
3 screwed to rail using wood buttons
4 fitted into groove in rail

Corner joints
Leg and rail
a) tongue and groove
b) dowelled
c) notched
d) mitred tenon

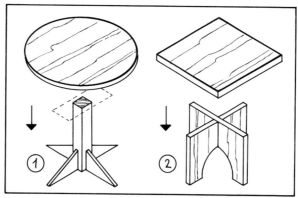

Table legs
1 central pedestal, gives more knee space
2 crossed boards, can be taken apart

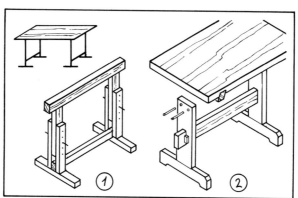

Trestles with loose table tops are easily assembled and taken apart.
1 trestle, height adjustable
2 trestle with joint of stretcher keyed to leg. The legs and table top are joined by dowels in the block under the table top

Table frames
1 diagonally crossed legs for outdoor use
2 tenoned rails. Table top attached to frame by wood buttons

Chairs

Chair constructions are
distinguished by the shape,
number and position of the legs;
the shape of the seat, the arms
and back; and the type of joints
used. Usually hardwoods such as
beech, oak or mahogany are
used. Because chairs are used so
much, the joints between the rails
and the legs must be strong and
well constructed.
A useful rule of thumb; the
higher the seat, the smaller its
area. Together the measurements
add up to approximately 950mm
(37in).

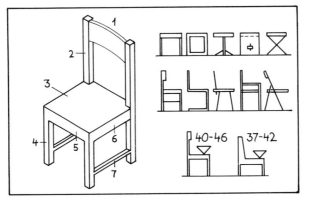

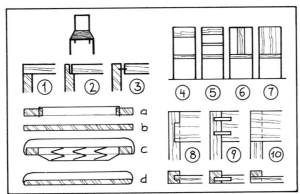

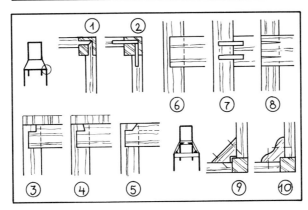

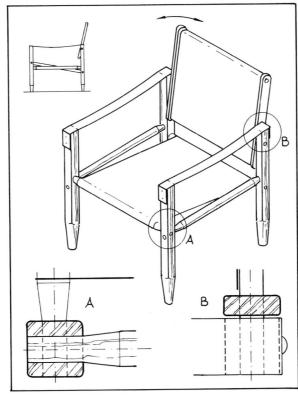

A

B

Parts of a chair
1 backrest
2 back legs
3 seat
4 leg
5 apron
6 side rail
7 side stretcher

Diagrams to the right show
various chair and stool
constructions

Chair
1 on frame
2 recessed into frame
3 fitted into side of frame
a) wicker b) plank
c) upholstered, spring interior
d) upholstered, foam
4–7 Backrests
joints between backrest and back
legs:
 8 tongue and groove
 9 dowelled
10 rebated

Joints: frame to leg
1 mitred tenon
2 dowelled

Haunches
3 straight
4 slanting forward
5 slanting backward

Haunch joints
6   concealed
7   dowelled
8   wedged
9/10 strengthening blocks

Canvas chair
Made up of joined rods that can
be taken apart. The principle is
that the bars are held together by
pressure (detail A). The parts of
the frame of this armchair are
held together by the canvas seat
and back, which are stretched on
cord. The arms are made of
strips of leather. Two strong
bolts attach the chair frame to
the movable backrest (detail B).

35

2 Furniture joints

KLAUS PRACHT · JENS BECKER

Introduction

This chapter deals with the most important woodworking joints and illustrates how they are made. First of all, we will discuss the tools and machines necessary for cutting the wood, and the additional tools, such as clamps, required for assembling the joints. Both permanent joints and knock-down fittings are shown from traditional dovetail joints to modern metal fittings.

Wood is a living material, and its structure and characteristics must always be borne in mind. The correct choice of joint can improve the value of a piece of furniture just as a wrong choice can have the opposite effect. When you are making a piece of furniture it is always worth being aware of the variety of joints possible.

Tools

Tools for measuring and marking out

Precise workmanship is only possible if measuring and marking out instruments are used. They help to transfer information from the plan to the workpiece.

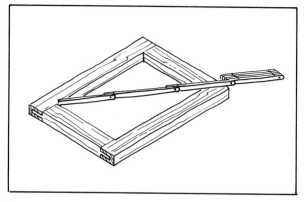

A **metre rule** is marked in millimetres. Total length: 2m (79in)

Equal diagonals inside a frame prove that it is right-angled.

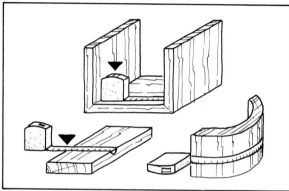

A **steel measuring tape**, usually 2m (79in) long. This is made of spring steel and winds in automatically. It is suitable for inside measurements and for measuring curved components.

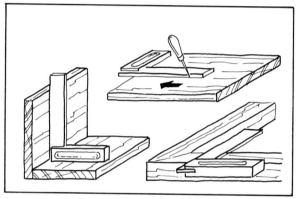

A **try-square** is used for marking out and assembling right angles, both horizontally and vertically.
1 testing that surfaces are square to each other
2 marking out

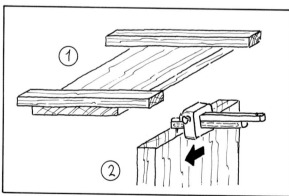

1 **Winding strips,** made of teak (as this does not warp). These are used to test planed surfaces. If the surface is level, the top edges of the winding strips can be seen to be parallel.
2 A **marking gauge** consists of two adjustable parallel pieces of wood with marking pins. It is used to mark out lines parallel to the edge of the wood.

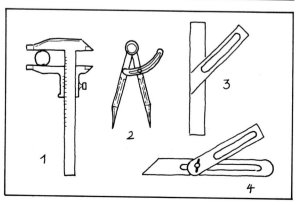

1 **Veneer calipers** are used for precise measurements, e.g. boreholes.
2 **Wing compasses** are used for marking out and transferring curves and radii.
3 A **mitre square** has set angles of 45° and 135°.
4 An adjustable **sliding level** is used to mark out and test angles.

Hand-tools

In order to work wood it is
essential to have very sharp tools
that can be re-sharpened
whenever necessary.
It is a good investment for the
amateur woodworker to have a
set of good quality tools. These
don't have to be new, as long as
they are in good condition.

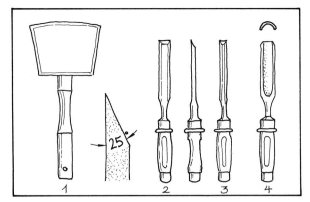

Cutting tools
1 carpenter's mallet
2/3 chisels of different widths;
common sizes; 6mm ($\frac{1}{4}$in),
10mm ($\frac{3}{8}$in), 16mm ($\frac{5}{16}$in),
20mm ($\frac{3}{4}$in). Cutting edge 25°
4 firmer gouge for hollowing
out

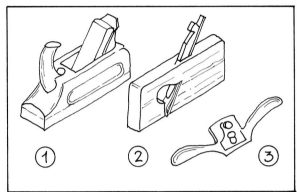

Planes
1 smoothing plane, for
smoothing up surfaces and
planing end grain
2 rebate plane, to cut rebates, e.g.
in doors
3 spokeshave, to smooth curves

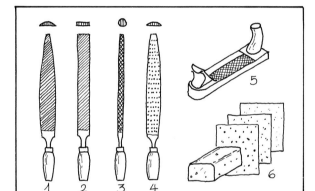

Files and rasps
1 half-round file
2 flat file
3 round or rat-tail file
4 half-round rasp
5 surform tool
6 abrasive paper, grit size:
coarse: 30–60
medium: 80–100
fine: 120–180
extra fine: 220–320

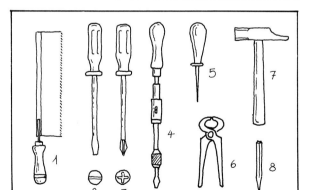

Small tools
1 backsaw
2 screwdriver, straight head
3 screwdriver, Phillips head
4 yankee screwdriver
5 awl
6 pincers
7 hammer, 200g (7oz)
8 nail punch

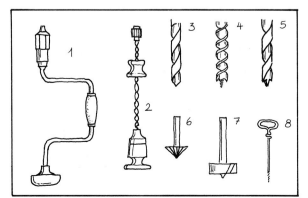

Drills
1 carpenter's ratchet brace
2 Archimedian drill
3 twist drill
4 Jennings pattern auger bit
5 brad point drill
6 rose countersink bit
7 Forstner pattern bit
8 gimlet

Machine tools

Using a machine saves time and energy. This is perhaps not so important for the amateur woodworker, but the use of machines makes better and more precise workmanship possible. The most versatile basic tool for the amateur is the electric drill. Anyone who wants to take complete advantage of the various possibilities available should buy a drill with at least two speeds and with a wide range of attachments.

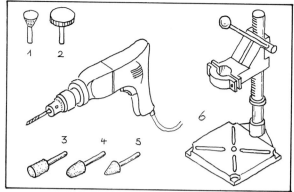

Portable electric drill, attachments:
1   rasp, e.g. for pins and dovetails
2   combination rasp, e.g. for grooves and rebates
3–5 router bits, used as file
6   drill stand, for worktop use, with adjustable collar to take different types of drill

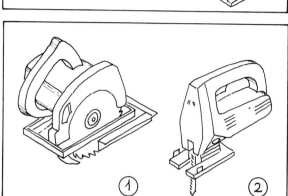

1 Portable circular saw cutting depth up to 65mm (2½in), input up to 700 watts, blade adjustable up to 45°, with parallel fence.

2 Jig saw with safety guard adjustable for cutting bevels, useful for rounded and curved cuts.

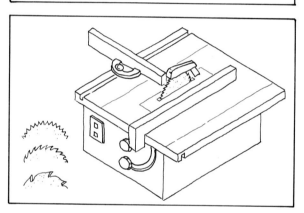

Circular saw, (fixed), with motor and work top.
Height of blade adjustable, parallel and bevelled fences adjustable; used for cutting mitres etc.
Input: aprox. 800–1,200 watts.

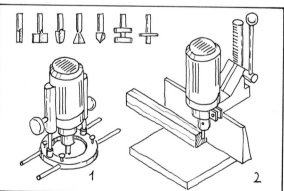

3 Routers
1   portable vertical routing machine
2   portable vertical routing machine with table stand or special stand. Routing and mortizing attachments are available.

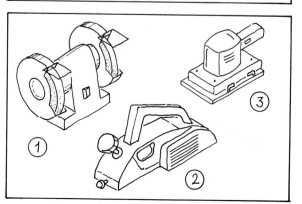

Smoothing tools
1   double-ended grinder, e.g. to sharpen chisel or plane blades and bits
2   electric plane for quick removal of waste wood and surface smoothing
3   orbital sander for smoothing and sanding large planed surfaces

Clamps and vices

Clamps and vices are used when sawing and drilling, planing and carving, as well as for holding glued workpieces together to dry. Workbenches themselves are very useful holding tools. They are stable and suitable for both large or small workpieces, but they are stationary, of course.

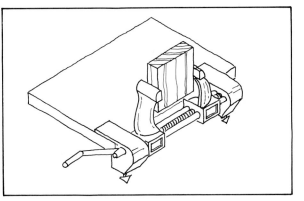

The **Zyliss vice**, suitable for light work, is fixed to the bench top with two clamps and consists of a handle, a spindle and two jaws.

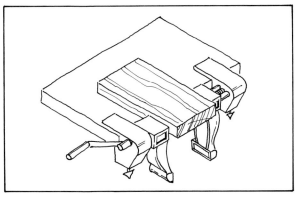

If the jaws are tipped downwards, the work can be held, e.g. for planing.

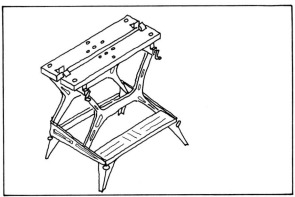

The **Workmate workbench** is collapsible, easy to transport and suitable for most kinds of joinery and assembly work.

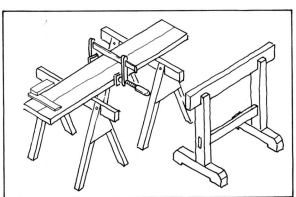

Trestles are ideal for use as a sawhorse, for supporting large boards or as a workbench. They are light, compact, relatively cheap and the height can be adjusted on some.

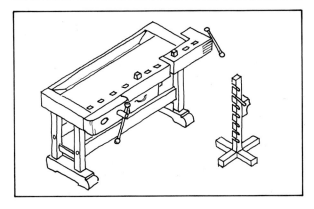

The **woodworker's bench** is suitable for holding boards, planks, battens or squared timber. It is usually equipped with a drawer for small tools. An upright bench leg is sometimes necessary when working with large boards.

Materials

Properties of wood

Wood is a very popular material for furniture. As an organic material it has a high tensile strength in relation to its weight, and favourable physical properties. It is also easy to work.

The elasticity of a piece of wood is a decisive factor in its ability to support. It has long fibres and bends under stress. It is therefore very suitable for frames, e.g. for seating.

The **cutting quality** of a piece of wood depends partly on its moisture content.

● Softwood has a high tensile strength in relation to its density, and does not warp much; prices are lower than for hardwood.
● Hardwood is heavier and not as easy to work as softwood.

Hardness of timber:
1 very soft: lime, poplar, willow
2 soft: birch, alder, spruce, pine, larch
3 medium hard: ash, plane, elm
4 hard: maple, oak, beech, walnut, cherry
5 very hard: durmast oak, hornbeam, pitch pine
6 extremely hard: box, olive

Elasticity:
1 very little elasticity: pine, poplar
2 little elasticity: alder, hornbeam, larch, fir
3 medium elasticity: birch, lime, elm, walnut
4 much elasticity: red beech, oak, spruce, pear
5 very much elasticity: ash, teak, yew

Cutting quality:
1 very easy to cut: spruce, fir
2 easy to cut: pine, larch, oak, lime, alder
3 moderately easy to cut: red beech, walnut, chestnut
4 difficult to cut: ash, maple
5 very difficult to cut: hornbeam, birch, elm
6 extremely difficult to cut: yew, plane, cherry

Softwood is easier to glue and easier to work than hardwood. Hardwood is better suited to heavy use than softwood, but is popular for furniture.

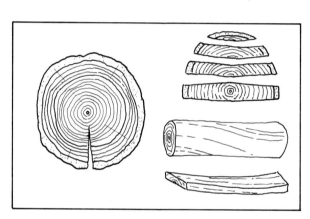

The quality of timber depends on the growth of the tree. Since it is a natural material, it is exposed to environmental influences, e.g. storm, frost, heat and damage by animals. It swells or shrinks according to the temperature and humidity, or it can grow spirally. This swelling and shrinking is known as warping. This is an important factor to consider when working timber.

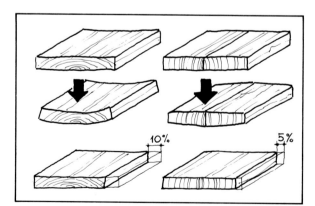

As a rule of thumb: shrinkage on drying in the direction of the grain = 0,1%
in the direction of the medullary rays = 5%
in the direction of the annual rings = 10%

Properties of wood

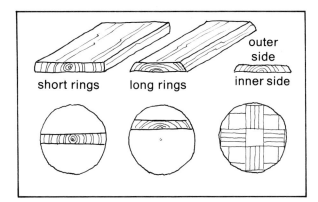

When choosing wood, that with the closest rings is preferable. Boards with widely spaced annual rings are most likely to warp. Also, note the difference between the outer and the inner side of a board: the outer side (towards the bark) becomes hollow when drying, the inner (towards the heart) becomes convex.

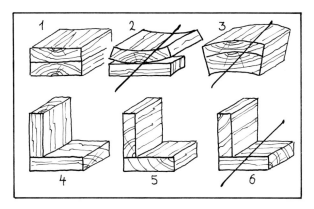

Wood must be glued according to the cut used.
1 correct:
   sapwood to sapwood or heartwood to heartwood
2 incorrect:
   crosscut to grain wood
3 incorrect:
   heartwood to sapwood
4/5 correct:
   same direction of shrinkage
6 incorrect:
   grain wood on crosscut wood

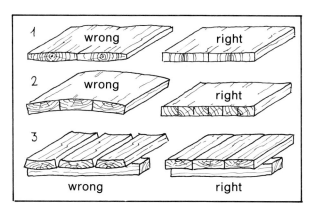

1 The pith should be cut out of a board to remove the tension.
2 The inner and outer sides of boards should always be glued alternately.
3 When boards are joined at right angles to another, the inner (rounded) side should always be on top, so that the joints remain closed.

Defects in timber and how to deal with them

Checks due to incorrect seasoning:
   glue small checks:
   cut along large checks first.

Knots, tight or loose:
   bore out large knots and glue in piece of wood as replacement.

Spirally grown timber:
   boards cut from this wood are unsuitable for furniture.

Resin galls:
   scratch out the resin and fill with stopper.

Commonly available prepared wood

There are so many different types of prepared wood available – sawn timber, boards and planks, roughly sawn, planed or sanded – that there is normally no problem in finding the right wood at a timber merchant. There is a huge variety of uses for solid wood in furniture construction, e.g. for seating: legs and posts, rails and stretchers, bars and backrests; for carcase constructions: frames and plinths, battens and edges, sides, fronts and backs of carcases, etc.

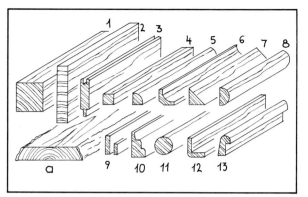

Commercially available prepared wood
a) waney-edged plank.
1   sawn timber, planed and in various sizes
2   boards, common widths 100–279mm (4–11in), thicknesses 12–36mm ($\frac{1}{2}$–1$\frac{1}{2}$in)
3   tongue and groove boards
4–13 solid wood battens, wood for frames, special mouldings

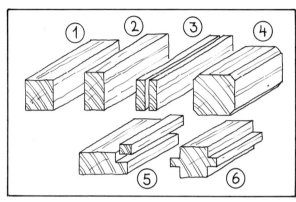

Squared timber
1 squared timber, sides 60–180mm (2$\frac{1}{4}$–7in)
2 plank, thicknesses 40–100mm (1$\frac{1}{2}$–4in)
3 boards, thicknesses 10–40mm ($\frac{1}{2}$–1$\frac{1}{2}$in)
4 shaped timber, chamfered
5 frame timber, rebated, with beading to hold panel
6 frame timber, rebated on both sides

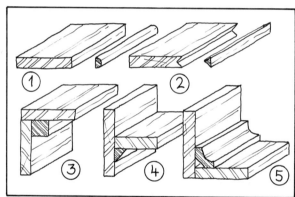

Beading and battens
1 rounded
2 triangular beading, flush fitting
3 squared batten used in joint
4 triangular batten as support
5 hollow moulded batten to keep dust free or to cover join

Uses of squared timber
1 bridle, or open mortise and tenon joint
2 as frame joint
3 as corner of mortized frame
4 nailed joint board and post

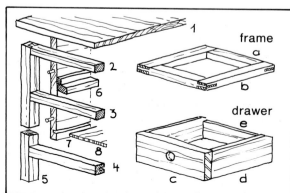

Carcase constructions with posts
1   top
2/3 bearing rails
4   plinth frame
5   post
6   runner and side rail
7   side panel
8   bottom
● Parts of frame
a) rail
b) stile
● Parts of drawer
c) drawer front
d) drawer side
e) drawer back

Veneers and manufactured boards

As boards made of solid wood tend to shrink, warp or split, so-called manufactured boards are becoming increasingly popular. These will keep their shape over long periods even if they are several square metres in size. Popular types are blockboard, laminboard, chipboard and plywood; plywood being used most frequently. They are good value for money and adequate for most types of furniture, but they are also very heavy and sensitive to moisture. Blockboard and laminboard are much lighter, more stable (screws are difficult to pull out) but also more expensive. Rounded components can be formed from plywood made of several thin layers.

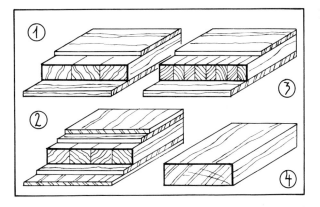

Blockboard and laminboard consist of two veneered layers sandwiching a centre of glued strips of solid wood.
1 blockboard, 3-ply
2 blockboard, 5-ply
3 laminboard
4 solid wood as comparison
   Thicknesses; 16, 19, 22mm ($\frac{5}{8}$, $\frac{3}{4}$, $\frac{7}{8}$in)

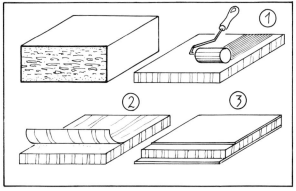

Chipboard is made by glueing and compressing wooden chips. Its smooth surface is suitable for:
1 painting
2 veneers (always on both sides)
3 coating (film or synthetic facing)
   Thicknesses: 10, 13, 16, 19, 22, 34mm ($\frac{3}{8}$, $\frac{1}{2}$, $\frac{5}{8}$, $\frac{3}{4}$, $\frac{7}{8}$, $1\frac{1}{2}$in)

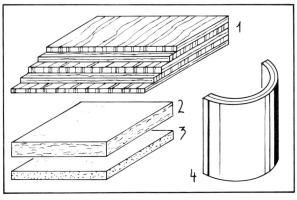

Plywood
1 5-ply, veneer layers glued with the grain of each layer at right angles to the next

Hardboard
2 soft
   Thicknesses: 6–12mm ($\frac{1}{4}$–$\frac{1}{2}$in), for insulation against noise and heat loss
3 hard
   Thicknesses: 1.6–8mm ($\frac{1}{16}$–$\frac{5}{16}$in), for back panels and drawer bottoms
4 rounded, 2-ply, glued

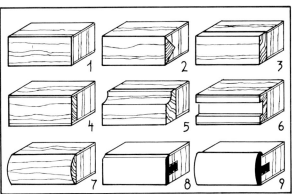

Edge coverings protect edges
1   veneer edging strip
2/4 solid wood
5   moulded edge covering
6   grooved edge covering
7   rounded edge covering
8/9 plastic edge covering

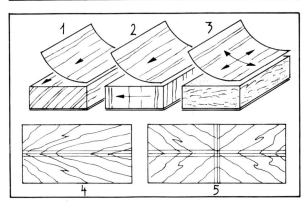

Veneers are thin sheets of cut wood, approx. 0.8mm ($\frac{1}{32}$in) thick. The whole surface is glued to the material covered, e.g. chipboard.
1 on solid wood, grain directions parallel
2 on blockboard, grains at right angles
3 on chipboard, grain in any direction
4 book matched veneer
5 reverse diamond veneer

Woodworking joints

Joints for widening boards and corner joints

The choice of woodworking joint is influenced by technical and economic factors.

● It is essential to consider the way in which the wood has grown.

● Joints for widening are used to make larger surfaces (e.g. shelves and panels).

● Corner joints join different planes, e.g. shelves and the sides of bookcases or cupboards.

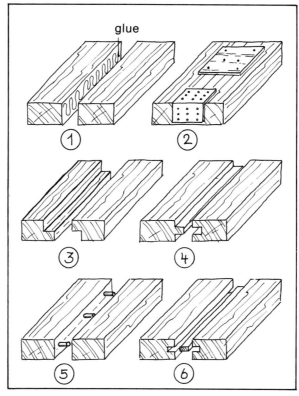

Joints for widening
1 glued butt joints
2 with metal reinforcing plates, flat or right-angled
3 rebated, large glued surface
4 tongue and groove, e.g. floor boards
5 dowelled, for heavy wear
6 tongue and groove, with loose tongue

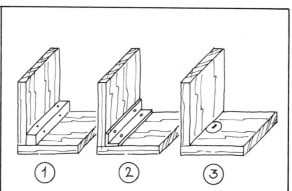

Simple corner joints
1 butt joint strengthened with solid wood corner block, nailed, or preferably screwed
2 strengthened with L-shaped metal strip
3 strengthened with removable metal plate, concealed

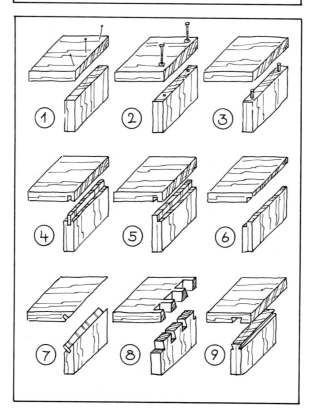

Traditional corner joints
1 dovetail nailing
2 screwed
3 dowelled
4 tongue and groove, with loose tongue
5 groove, with rebated tongue
6 double rebated
7 mitred, with loose tongue
8 dovetail, only with solid wood
9 dovetail housing, only with solid wood

Frame construction joints

Frame joints can be made with wood or with metal, visible or concealed, while end joints may be halving, grooves or finger joints. Metal plates can also be used just as well. However, end joints should only be used when it is not possible to use a continuous piece of timber, e.g. in curved frames where the wood would otherwise be too short. Post constructions make strong corner joints. Frames and panels may be made in very different ways.

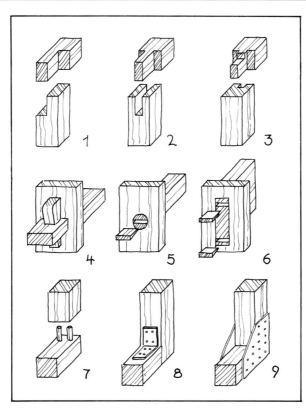

Stool- and flat frame joints
1 halving
2 corner bridle
3 mortise and tenon, square haunch

Stool-frame joints
4 mortise and tenon, with removable key
5 spigot, with wedge
6 whole of frame end serves as tenon, wedged

Flat frame joints
7 dowelled
8 with right-angled metal plate
9 with flat metal plates

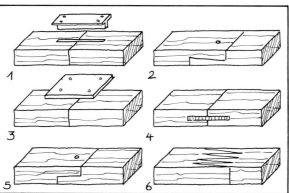

End joints
1 grooved and joined with T-shaped metal plate
2 scarf
3 screwed plywood plate
4 tongue and groove, with loose tongue
5 half lap
6 finger

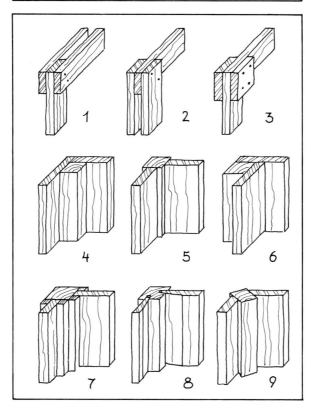

Simple frame constructions
1–3 nailed boards

Post and panel constructions
4 post inside, concealed
5 post at corner, visible
6 post at centre panel, e.g. cupboard

Frames and panels
7 panels held by beading
8 panels held in grooved frame
9 frame diagonal, panels joined by dowels.

Adhesives

Types of glue

There are different types of
adhesive used for glueing wood
and manufactured board in
different circumstances:
● PVA glue, e.g. for butt joints
● contact adhesives for glueing
  veneer

1 PVA glue is available ready-
  mixed in containers.
2 all-purpose glues are
  transparent, waterproof and
  elastic
3 contact adhesives in tubes
4 expoy resin glues, consisting of
  hardener and resin, suitable for
  high stress joints.

● Use a brush to glue small
  surfaces
● Spread glue over large
  surfaces with a comb,
  preferably not made of metal.

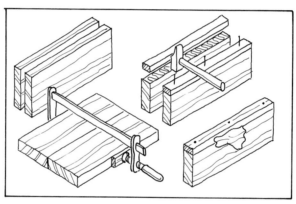

Apply pressure to the glued parts
using cramps and scrap wood for
a long enough period (e.g. 1–3
hours, according to the
manufacturer's instructions).
Excess glue can be wiped off
with a damp cloth while still wet.

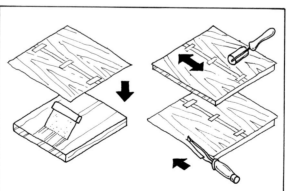

Glue should always be applied to
the whole surface of veneer
sheets, and the joined surfaces
then be pressed together with a
roller. Remove the veneer overlap
with a sharp chisel when the glue
is set.

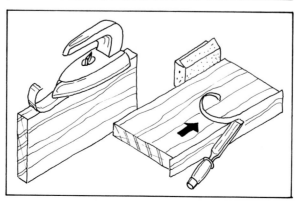

Edging strips are coated with a
glue that melts when heat is
applied, and are ironed on. (Set
the iron at 'cotton'.) The overlap
is removed with a chisel or a
special knife, and then sanded.

Using adhesives

Place the boards together in the position in which they are to be glued. To do this it is essential to know about the characteristics of wood (warping).

For wide components of solid wood, it is best to use narrow boards with the annual rings approx. at right angles to the frames to prevent warping.

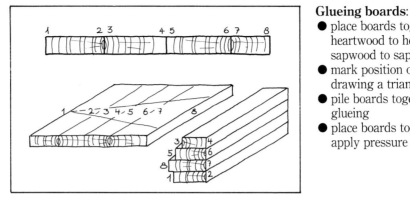

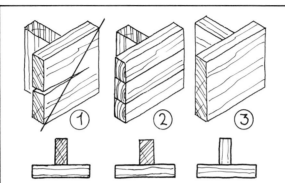

Glueing boards:
- place boards together heartwood to heartwood, sapwood to sapwood
- mark position of boards by drawing a triangle
- pile boards together for glueing
- place boards together and apply pressure

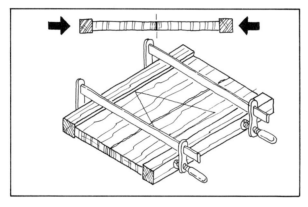

Corner joints
1 incorrect: long grain against cross grain; wood may split
2 poor: several narrow boards all with inner surface facing outwards
3 correct: cross grain against cross grain; parts move in the same direction

Scrap wood is used to prevent harm to the workpiece when applying pressure. It is best to glue both surfaces when working with chipboard.

Pressure must be applied evenly. Use large pieces of scrap wood and enough clamps.

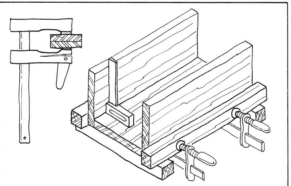

When flat battens are glued onto each other it is often enough to use wood clamps with tightening levers.

When glueing box constructions always use a try-square to check and correct right angles.

two short clamps used together

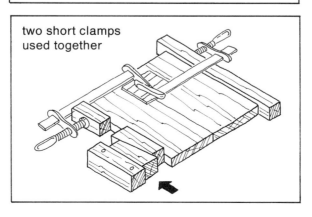

Short clamps can be used together. Wedges can also be used between pieces of scrap wood that have been screwed together.

Halving

Halving (also called half laps) is not a high stress joint, but unlike a mortise, it is easy to make.

A **try-square and marking gauge** are used for marking out. The width and depth of the cut depend on the width and depth of the second piece of wood.
For half lap joints, the components should have the same width and depth as far as possible.

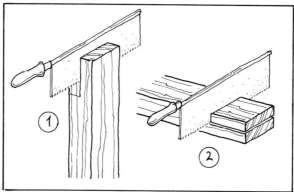

Saw down and across the grain with a tenon saw:
1 make the initial cut across the end grain and saw down the grain.
2 cut the 'shoulder' at a right angle to the workpiece and remove.
The pencil mark should still be just visible!

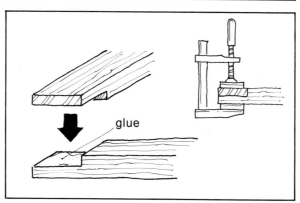

glue

Before glueing the parts, try them together, trimming with a chisel if necessary.
Apply glue to all surfaces, clamp together using scrap wood for protection and adjust the angle if necessary.

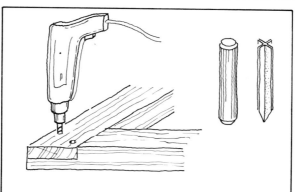

Wooden dowels or alloy star pins can be used to strengthen the joint. Dowel overlap can be removed with a chisel; alloy star pins are driven right into the wood.

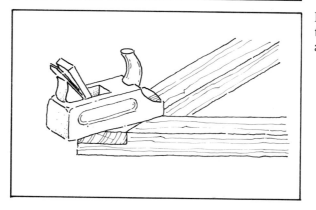

Plane the corners smooth and then sand them (grit size 100) and all the other edges.

Cross halving

Corner and cross joints of either boards, battens or even posts can be joined by cross halving. A piece half the depth of each component is cut out from the face of one part of the frame and the back of the other, taking care not to cut into the face of the upright frame.

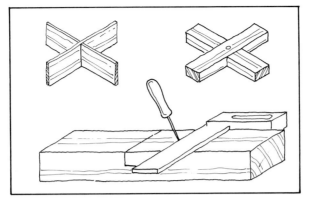

Mark out with a try-square and marking knife or pencil.
Half the thickness of each of the two components must be cut away.

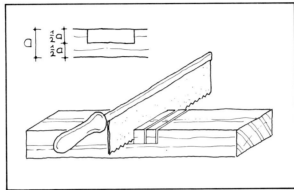

Make cuts with a tenon saw to mark the width of the trench. The gauge line must always be visible. Guide lines should also be cut in the centre of the trench.

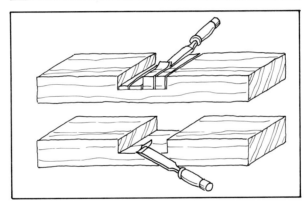

Chisel out the waste from both edges towards the centre. Cut out the bottom of the trench carefully, making sure that it is perfectly flat.

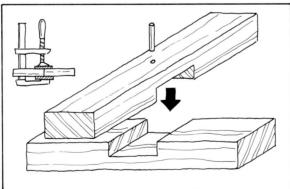

When the two pieces have been successfully tested together, they can be **glued**. The fit is correct when both pieces stay together before glueing.
Apply the glue evenly, particularly against the shoulder (end grain).

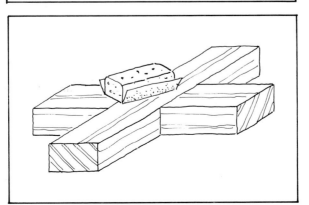

If there is any **overlap** the joint must be planed, otherwise sanding will be enough.

Bridle joints, mortise and tenon joints

Bridle joints

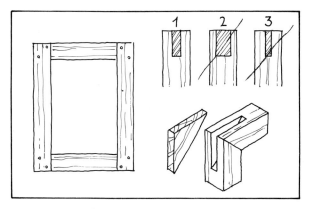

The thickness of the trench or slot should be about a third of the thickness of the component (1). The trench in (2) is too wide and in (3) too narrow. Bottom right: example of a mitred corner joint with a triangular tongue.

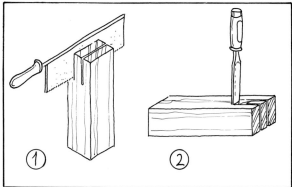

Cutting trenches
1 Cut the width and depth of the trench with a tenon saw.
2 Then chisel half way through the trench, turn the member and repeat from the other side.

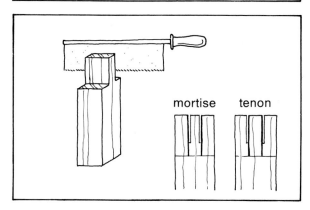

When cutting the **tenon**, saw along the outer side of the marking line. Compare diagrams.

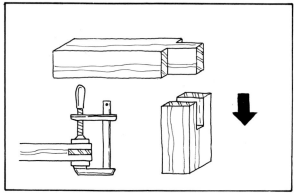

Test and trim the components for fit before glueing, then glue and clamp them together.
In a closed frame the right angles of all four corners can be tested by placing a piece of wood diagonally from one corner to the opposite. The angles are correct if the diagonal distances are the same.

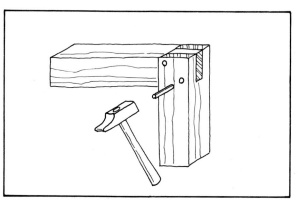

The joints can be **strengthened** by adding wooden dowels when the glue has set. It is best to use two dowels set diagonally. Plane and sand the surface smooth.

Mortise and tenon joints

Careful workmanship is vital if constructions made of solid wood, such as chairs, frames or ladder rungs are to last. Blind or stopped mortise and tenon joints are concealed (e.g. for tables). Full or through mortise and tenon joints may also be wedged, which makes them strong and stable.

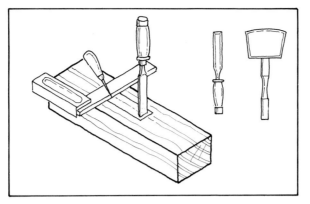

Marking out
The mortise should be one third the width of the member. Use a try-square and a marking knife for marking out.

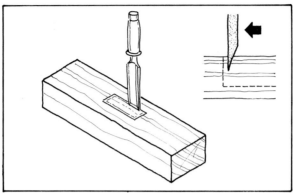

Cutting the mortise
Make the initial cuts by holding the chisel absolutely upright, with the blade parallel to the marking line.

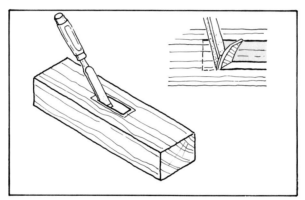

First **chisel out** the depth of the mortise by cutting off thin shavings vertically up the side lines. The chisel must cut absolutely vertically. The bevelled edge of the chisel should always face the side lines.

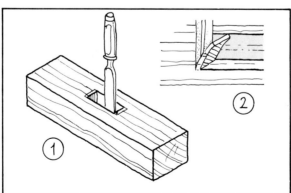

When the mortise has been roughly chiselled out, it has to be trimmed to the exact size. Make the tenon as described for bridle joints.

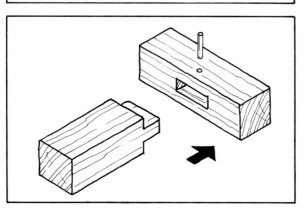

Dowelling
The tenon should fit tightly into the mortise when tested. Glue the joint and then strengthen it with a dowel or lease pin.

Rebate joints

Rebates can be made by adding a narrower piece of wood to the original component or by planing or cutting a piece off the edge of a component, either along the grain or across it.

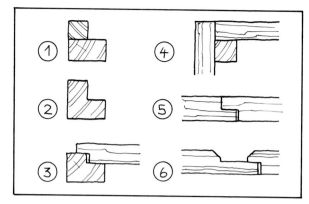

Rebate
1 two components, glued together
2 rebated frame
3 corner, rebate joint
4 rebate joint using additional glued block, e.g. back of cupboard
5 rebate joint
6 moulding, rebate joint

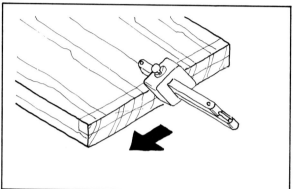

At the **marking out** stage, the width and depth of the rebate are marked onto the board. The cut-out piece should be no thicker than half the thickness of the board.

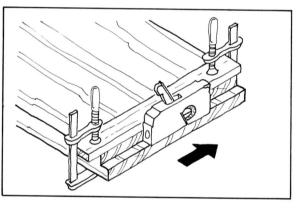

A batten is used as a guide for the **rebate plane**. Always plane from the outer corner inwards, to avoid splitting at the ends.

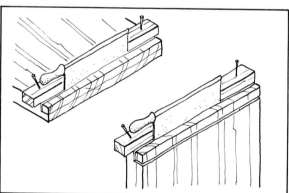

When **sawing rebates** with a tenon saw, a batten can also be used as a guide; in this case it can be firmly nailed in place. Hold the tenon saw vertically for the whole length of the cut, and don't tilt it at all.

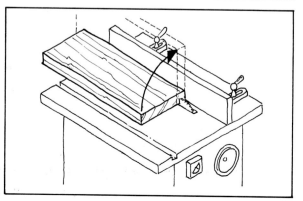

Cutting rebates with a circular saw is the quickest and neatest method. The board is first held horizontally and then vertically over the blade. The size of the rebate is determined by the height of the saw blade.

Tongue and groove joints

The tongue may be continuous or comprise of different parts, if it is not to be seen from the edge. It is either cut out of a component or a separate piece of wood is used. Plywood is the best wood for this.

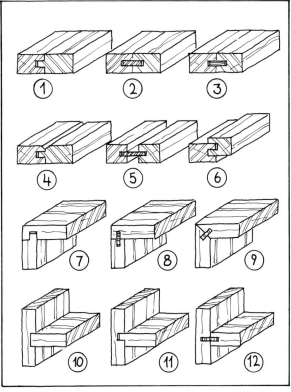

Tongue and groove joints for widening
1 tongue and groove joint for floorboards, doors, panels
2 spline, with separate tongue (along the grain)
3 spline, with separate cross grain tongue to take vertical pressure
4 tongue and groove, bevel-edged boards
5 spline, with wide tongue
6 staggered tongue and groove joint, for doors, ceiling panels

Tongue and groove corner joints
7 tongue cut out of member
8 with separate tongue (cross grain)
9 tongue through mitre joint
10 trench, full thickness of board (dado joint)
11 trench for tongue on one side of board (dado and rebate)
12 with separate tongue (cross grain)

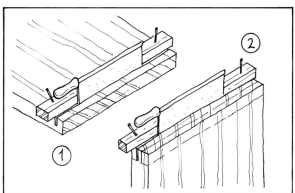

Trenches are cut across a board with a **tenon saw and a chisel**, using a batten as a fence. Thin strips of plywood are used as separate tongues.

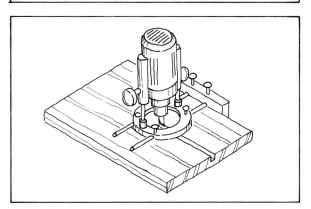

Trenches can be cut much better and more quickly using a **router**. It is a good idea to test the depth and width of the trenches on a piece of scrap wood first.

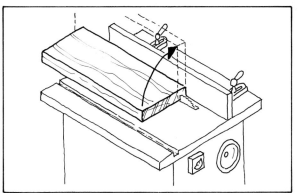

Depending on the joint chosen, the board is held either horizontally or vertically over a **circular saw blade**. A blade width of 4–5mm ($\frac{3}{16}$in) is usually sufficient for cutting a reasonable sized groove.

Dowel joints

Dowel joints without a jig

Dowelled joints are easy to make and are becoming more popular than tongue and groove or mortise and tenon joints. Holes for the dowels are bored into both components with the same tool. Dowels can be used in butt joints or even in mitre joints.

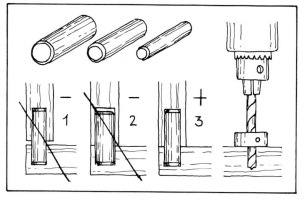

Dowels are made from beech rods.
The diameter of the dowel should not be more than one-third of the thickness of the board.
The length of the dowel should be slightly less than the depth of the hole.
Adjustable stops are available for drills.

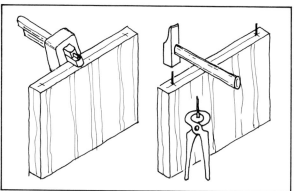

Marking out
A marking gauge is used to mark along the centre of the board.
The bore holes are marked with headless panel pins.

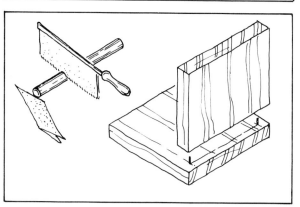

The **pins** should not protrude for more than 2–3mm ($\frac{1}{8}$in). They are then pressed against the second component, marking the exact position for the bore holes. This done, they are removed with pincers. The sawn-off dowelling has to be bevelled at the ends.

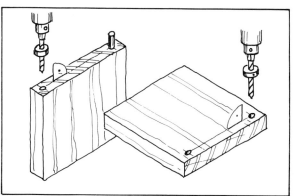

Use a **drill** with a centre point bit to bore the holes of the size required for the dowels in the boards.
Holes should not be bored more than two-thirds of the thickness of the face of the board.

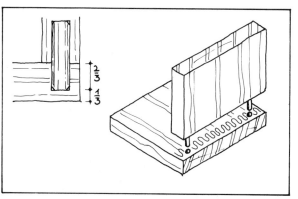

Before **assembly** the dowels are spread with glue and first driven into the hole of the cross cut wood. Then the two components can be pressed together. First glue the edges and then carefully press the workpieces together using a hammer and scrap wood.

Using a dowelling jig

Various types of dowelling jig are available commercially, all of which make it easier to bore holes precisely. This makes the marking out of the holes easier and prevents the drill slipping.

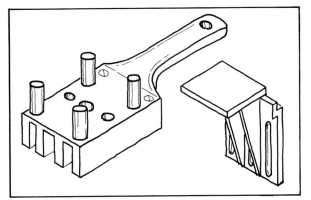

Plastic dowelling jigs
for three dowel sizes:
6, 8, 10mm ($\frac{1}{4}$, $\frac{5}{8}$, $\frac{3}{8}$in), with square fence

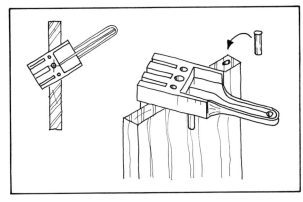

When the jig is held diagonally, the supports touch both sides of the board, automatically positioning the hole for the dowel to be bored in the centre.
When the holes have been bored the dowels are glued in place.

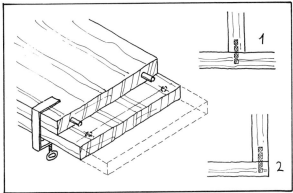

The holes to be bored are marked out with a marker gauge or a try-square onto the second component. The dowelled board is placed on the second board, a short distance from the end and with the edges exactly aligned, then the two boards are clamped together.

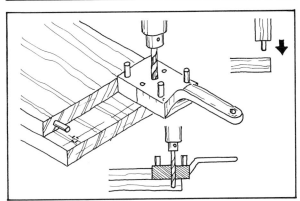

The marking on the side of the jig must align with the marking line for the holes to be bored. The set dowel in the first board fits into the jig, giving the exact position for boring.

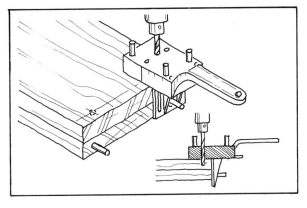

The **square fence** can also be used for boring dowel holes in the second component of a joint. A depth guide eliminates any possibility of boring through the board.

Comb and dovetail joints

Hand or machine-made dovetails are used whenever a strong pull or strain is expected. This traditional joint for box frame furniture, chests and drawers is attractive and durable, but also time-consuming to make.

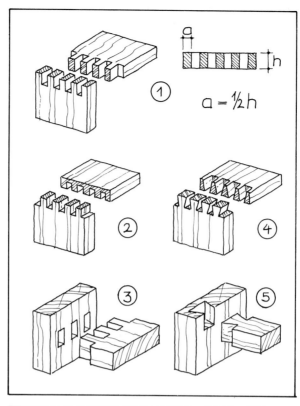

$$a = \tfrac{1}{2}h$$

Types

There are different types of comb and dovetail joints: they may be through or lapped, straight (comb) or dovetailed.

1 straight pins, comb or finger joint
2 lapped comb joint, for drawers
3 multiple mortise and tenon joint; the pins may be wedged, e.g. in furniture made of solid wood
4 dovetail joint; a strong joint that can be pushed or pulled
5 dovetail housing; used in frame construction

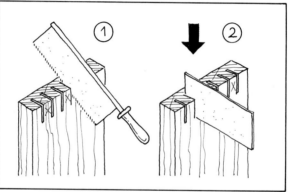

Cutting pins for a lapped comb joint:

1 first cuts
2 cuts completed using a chisel or scraper

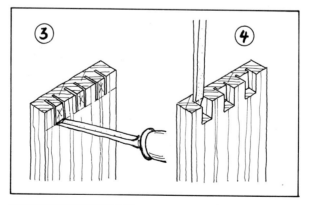

Chiselling out

1 chiselling the waste
2 trimming down to the gauge line

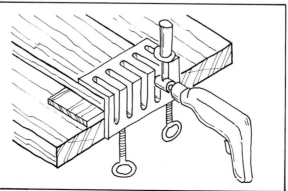

Using a jig

The finished piece is laid on the second component and the pins marked out against it. Using a jig and a power drill to make the pins saves time and produces a more exact fit.

Pin joints

Dovetail joints prevent boards from warping, but allow them to swell and shrink together. Workpieces joined by dovetails hold even without glueing, and no clamps need to be used to fit them.

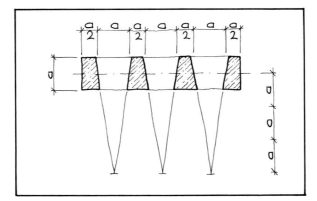

Marking out the pins
First mark out the pins at equal distances across the width of the board. The inner side of the board should always be on top.

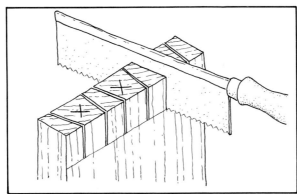

Cutting
Cut the pins vertically down to the depth required with a tenon saw. This depends on the size of the second board. The marking line should stay visible.

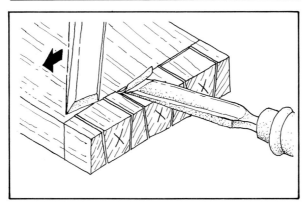

When making notches for removing the waste, hold the board firmly on the bench. Make cuts along the gauge line with a chisel.

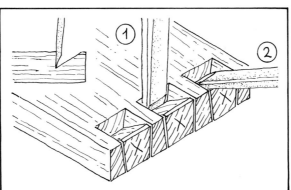

Removing the waste:
1 Hold the chisel vertically and cut into the timber.
2 Hold the chisel obliquely at the end of the board and cut the waste away (see diagram)

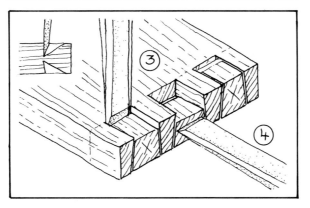

3 Turn the workpiece and follow the same procedure for the other side.
4 Remove the last bit and trim the ends.

Dovetails

The finished board with the pins is held in position against the second board and the pencil markings made around the pins.

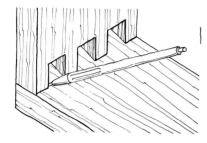

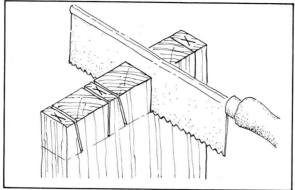

Cut the dovetails with a dovetail saw held carefully at the correct angle. Then cut away the waste at a right angle to the board surface.

Cut away the two outer 'pins' with a dovetail saw.

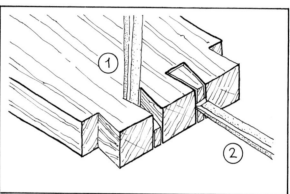

Remove the waste from the sockets in the same way as when cutting the pins: first cut into the timber, then chisel it out to the centre, turn the board and cut the waste away from the other side.

Trial assembly
When the dovetails have been neatly trimmed, give the unglued boards a trial assembly and make any corrections necessary.

Final assembly
Coat the pins carefully with glue and assemble the joint. When the glue has dried, plane the surfaces smooth from the outside inwards, and then sand them.

Wedged joints

Glued wedges

Glued wedges press the spigots apart, locking the joints. The pressure should always be against the end grain.

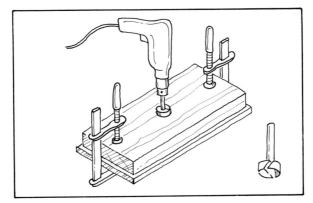

The spigot holes are bored with a twist drill or a Forstner bit. The hole should have exactly the same diameter as the spigot. A piece of scrap wood beneath the board prevents ragged edges round the exit hole.

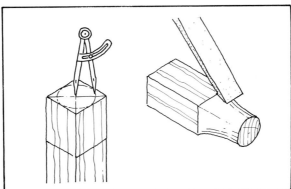

Marking out and preparing the spigot
Mark the diameter of the spigot into the end grain of the square end of a post. Chisel the sides of the component to a conical shape.

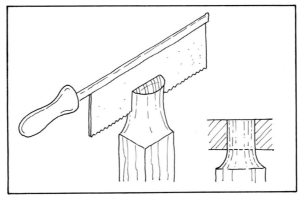

Cut a kerf two-thirds the length of the spigot to take the wedge. Fit the spigot into the hole in the board to test for fit.

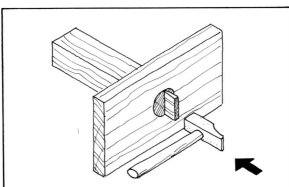

Wedging the spigot
After the edges have been glued, fit the spigot into the hole so that the wedge is at a right angle to the board.
Firmly secure a narrow hardwood wedge into the kerf, pressing the spigot against the sides of the hole. Glue the wedge too.

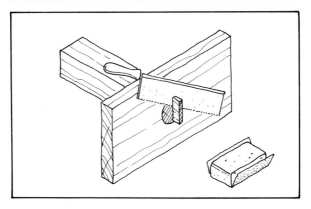

Trimming the wedge
When the glue has dried, saw off the remainder of the wedge that still protrudes. Plane the surface of the board smooth and then sand it.

Keyed joints

Keyed joints for rails have many advantages; for one thing they are extremely stable, for another they are easily dismantled. This is very important for furniture that has to be taken apart, e.g. bed frames. Keyed joints can be used either vertically or horizontally, and for narrow or wide components. The keys should be neither too short nor too angular. The tenon must be long enough not to crack from the pressure when the key is driven in.

Cut the shoulder of the tenon with a tenon saw, allowing for the size of the board and the protrusion necessary. Chisel out the hole for the key.

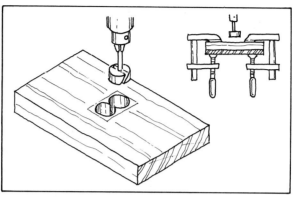

Make a mortise of exactly the same dimensions as the tenon in the board.

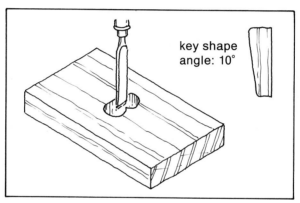

key shape angle: 10°

Chisel out the mortise from both sides.
Cut the key to the correct length, with a taper of about 10°.

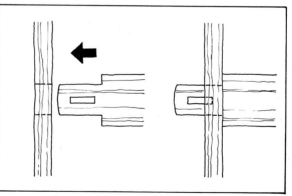

Fit the tenon through the mortise. The heyhole should be the right length so that the board and the tenon are pressed together when the key is driven in.

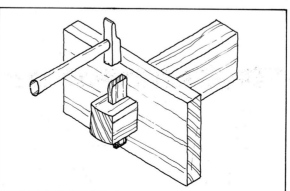

Drive the key into the hole with a hammer. The further down it is driven, the more secure the joint. It can be taken apart again by hammering in the opposite direction.

Screws and nails

Types

Screws are used for fixing metal fittings and for joining wooden parts, and are generally longer lasting than nails. They are available in various lengths and with various heads.

Nails are sold by weight, size and type. Depending on their use, they may be made of wood, iron, steel or brass. The shanks may be round, square or oval. Nails are available in lengths of 5–200mm ($\frac{3}{16}$–8in). Coarse, oval nails hold better than round ones.

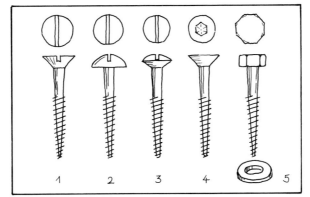

Screws for wood
1 countersunk head screw
2 round head screw
3 raised countersunk head screw
4 countersunk head screw with socket for an Allen key
5 hexagonal screw with washer

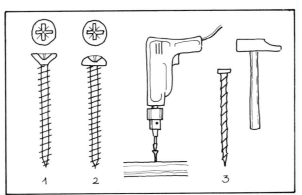

Quick screws
1 with countersunk head
2 with round head, useful for quick assembly, good holding power, can be screwed or unscrewed with an electric drill
3 nail with threaded shank, very good holding power

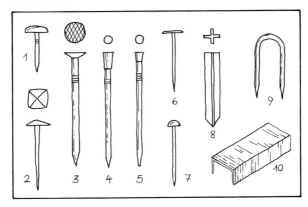

Nails
1 gimp pin
2 clout nail
3 round wire nail
4 oval wire nail
5 panel pin
6 tack
7 round headed panel pin
8 alloy star pin
9 round staple
10 square staples

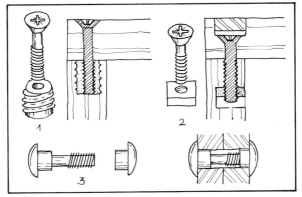

Cupboard fittings
1 fix cam, with brass bolt
2 countersunk screw with square nut
3 connecting bolt, e.g. used to join the sides of wall-mounted cupboards together

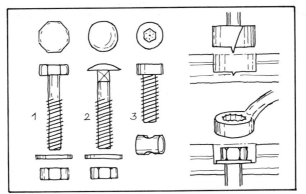

Nuts, bolts and machine screws
1 hexagonal bolt
2 coach bolt
3 bolt with socket for Allen key
When hexagonal bolts are to be recessed, holes are first bored with a Forstner bit and finally the bolts are tightened with a ring spanner.

Using screws

Screwed joints are much stronger than nailed joints. The strength of a screwed joint is dependent on the counter thread that is formed when the screw cuts into the wood. Thus wood screws should not be hammered or the pilot holes made too long. The thread of wood screws has a sharp edge, unlike that of screws for metal. Pilot holes can be made with a bradawl for small screws, and with a drill for larger screws. Conical recesses must be pre-formed for countersunk screws; round headed screws are screwed flush to the surface.

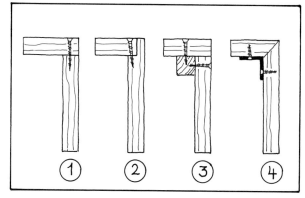

Methods of joining with screws
1 simple screwing, visible
2 diagonal screwing, with rebated corner joint
3 screwing with block
4 screwing from inside carcase, with metal plate, not visible from outside.

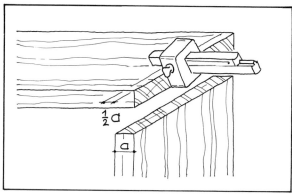

First mark out the position of the screw holes with the marking gauge. When using very long screws, bore a pilot hole with a fine bit (two-thirds the diameter of the screw).

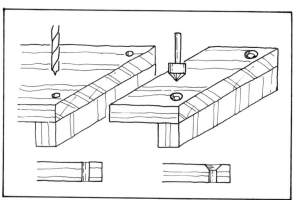

Then bore through the top board with a bit as wide as the screw shank. Form recesses for countersunk screws.

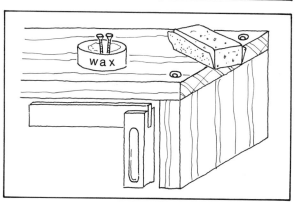

The boards and sides are assembled at an angle of 90°. Screws can be inserted more easily if they are first lubricated with wax.

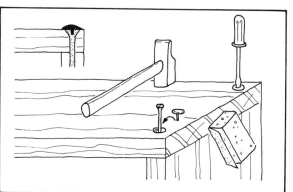

Screws can be hammered carefully into the holes to about a third of their total length. Only use screwdrivers with a blade that is wide enough. Screw heads may be covered with cups.

Nailing

Nailed joints are not as strong as screwed joints, but they are cheaper and quicker to make.

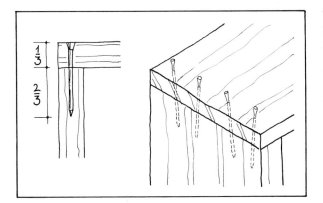

The length of a nail is more important than its thickness. A nail should be driven into the lower piece of wood up to two-thirds of its total length. Nails driven in at an angle (dovetail nailing) hold better!

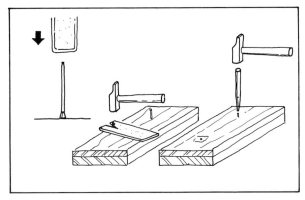

When nailing thin boards, the tip of the nail should be blunted first to prevent the wood splitting. Small nails can be held with a piece of slit cardboard. Always drive the head of a nail into the board.

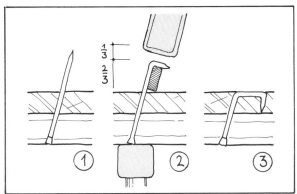

When nailing thin panels or battens, the nails are driven right through the wood, bent to form staples and nailed into the wood again.

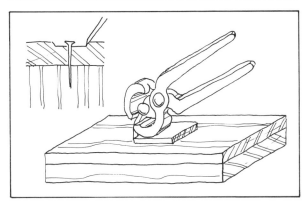

Before nails are pulled out it is sometimes advisable to chisel around the nail head. Always use scrap wood when pulling nails out with pliers to protect the surface of the wood from damage.

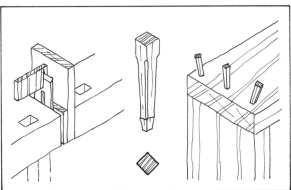

Wooden nails can be hand planed from birch or willow. They swell when damp, providing a very secure joint for solid wooden components.

Metal fittings

Metal plates

Metal plates are found in cheaper furniture. They are fixed with wood screws and therefore used in furniture which can be taken apart. Pre-fabricated parts are available for bed and frame constructions.

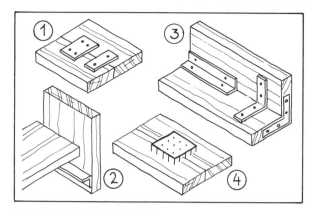

Plates
1 flat metal plates for widening boards
2/3 right angled plates for corner joints
4 nail plate, carpenter's joint, for bases

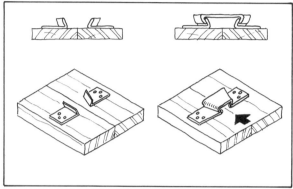

Metal wedges for widening boards consist of two angular pieces and one trapeze-shaped plate.
The trapeze plate is hammered over the two angular pieces and wedged into position.

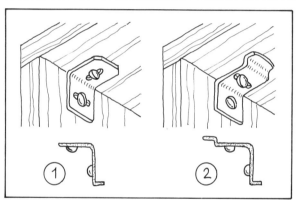

Metal plates
The slots in the metal plates allow for adjustment on assembly and for movement of the wood (swelling and shrinkage) after the plates have been screwed into place.
1 spiked
2 offset

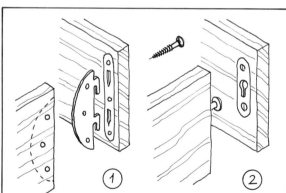

Bed fittings
1 recessed plate with hooks
2 with raised head screw that grips in the slit in the opposite metal plate
Both fittings may be taken apart by lifting upwards and outwards.

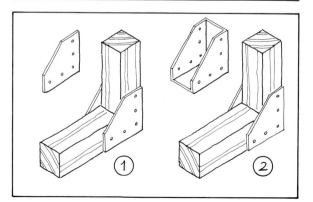

Metal reinforcing plates
for butt joints in frame constructions:
1 flat metal plates with pre-formed screw holes
2 frame corner, available from DIY shops in various sizes, galvanized, complete with screws

Knockdown fittings

Cupboards and shelves must be easy to transport and are therefore constructed in such a way that they can be taken apart easily. Cupboards can be fitted with special knock-down fittings for easy assembly and re-assembly. The joints are mounted either in or on the sides of the cupboards, centrally or towards the front. They are connected to the base vertically or horizontally. Important features of such fittings are their stability and their easy assembly.

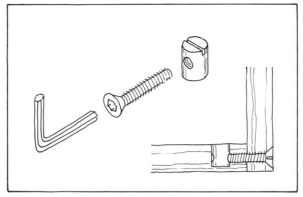

Countersunk head screws with sockets for an Allen key and cylinders are simple joints often found in self-assembly furniture kits. Using an Allen key, the screw is screwed into the thread of the cylinder from the outside.

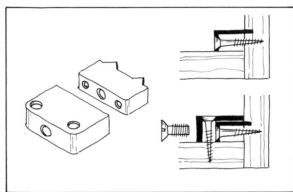

Corner jointing blocks consist of a lower part (spiked metal block) and a plastic upper part (cap). First the lower part is screwed onto one side of a cupboard. The cap is fitted over it and screwed first into the other board, and then secured with a screw into the first board.

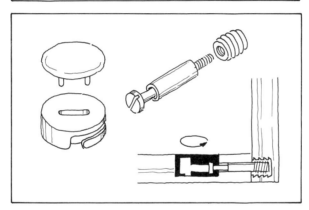

Fixing cams consist of a metal cylinder, a cap, screw and bolt. The joint is concealed, easily dismounted, and easy to fix with a screwdriver.

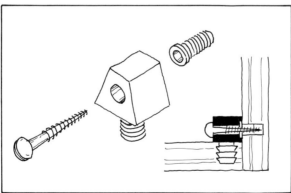

Chipboard insert, consisting of a plastic block with a bolt and a screw, not visible from outside, but projects into the inside of the cupboard.

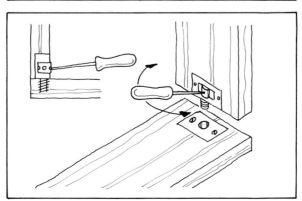

Traditional cupboard joint, consisting of one plate with a bolt and one with the female thread, both recessed.
A pin punch is used to screw the bolt tightly into the bottom plate; a classical knock-down joint.

3 Repairing furniture

KLAUS PRACHT · UTE FRISCH

Introduction

Constant use or a moment of carelessness can easily damage furniture such that repairs are necessary. Think of water stains on polished furniture, for example, or wobbly chair legs caused by being tipped too much.

However, the cost of having the damaged piece mended at a workshop are often so high that it is left undone. Therefore, repairing the furniture oneself seems the obvious solution.

This chapter consists of a systematic list of possible causes of damage and practical suggestions for repair.

Simple repairs to various parts of furniture are dealt with: treatment of tops, shelves and sides as well as restoring drawers, tables, chairs, beds, doors and tambour fronts and the respective locks and hinges.

In addition, specialized techniques and ways of treating surfaces are discussed.

Fixing tops

There are two basic types of tops fixed
to carcases:
a) removable, i.e. with particular joints
b) permanent, i.e. usually dowelled,
   screwed or rebated.
As old furniture almost always has
permanently fixed tops, we will deal
with these repairs here.

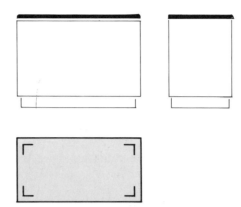

If a top has been removed to be repaired,
or if the old joint has loosened, this can
be repaired by glueing again.

The upper half of the adjacent diagram
demonstrates where the clamps are to be
positioned, according to the position of
the top.

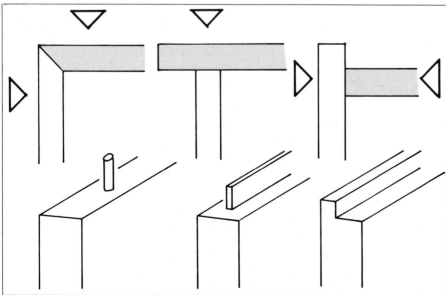

The lower half shows three possible
types of joint: dowel, tongue and rebate.
Broken-off dowels are removed with a
drill and replaced. Damaged tongues are
cut off and replaced by dowels.

The cleaned surfaces are given a thin coat of glue, the components fitted together exactly and the clamps fixed (using scrap wood to avoid pressure marks). Before the clamps are tightened, the position of the top should be given a final check.

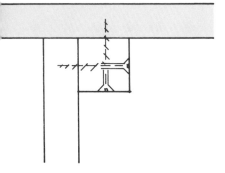

Instead of glueing or repairing the joints, the top can also be screwed onto the carcase via a wooden block with pilot screw holes. To do this, lay the piece of furniture on its side or upside down so that the screws can always be driven in downwards.

It is best to do any painting or varnishing, etc. beforehand, thus avoiding any chance of staining the old components.

Fitting shelves

Shelves are often overloaded and begin to sag. The shelves may be reinforced or new shelves can be added. Most DIY centres or timber merchants cut timber to the size required. A variety of shelf supports are also available (see bottom picture).

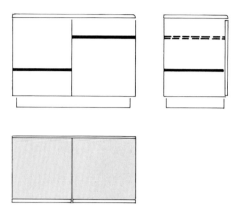

When shelves are to be added to a finished cupboard it is easiest to support them on metal or plastic shelf supports. Holes have to be bored for plastic studs. These should be marked, and a depth guide used to avoid boring right through the sides.

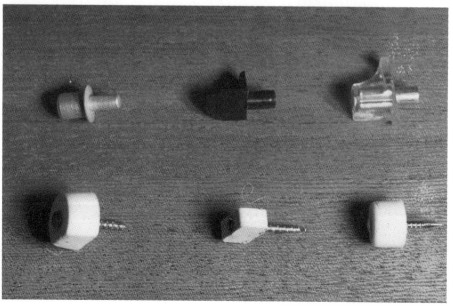

Shelves can also be fitted permanently using battens or blocks of wood (see next section 'fitting central panels'). A great number of different shelf supports are available. It is important to choose a type that will be held in its place by the shelf, i.e. that cannot fall out.

Fitting central panels

It is often necessary to fit a central panel into a cupboard, either to provide a better division of space or to support a sagging cupboard top. This is best done with veneered chipboard, blockboard, etc., that matches the rest of the cupboard, a hardwood batten and some screws.

Cut the batten to the right length, bore pilot holes in it and then screw it to the upper edge of the central panel. Now stand the cupboard upside down and mark out the position for the central panel. Bore pilot holes in the centre of the board and screw through from the outside. Finally screw the batten to the carcase.

If the central panel is to be removable, it can be held in position by plastic studs nailed into the top and bottom. Alternatively metal plates can be used that are slotted into the central panel and are thus concealed.
Using metal plates means that the panel is easier to fit into the cupboard, but making the slots in the panel takes up more time.

Stabilizing shelves

If the sides of a piece of furniture are no longer at the correct angle, or the furniture is unstable, often the back panel needs reinforcing. There are several ways of stabilizing a frame quickly and with little material.

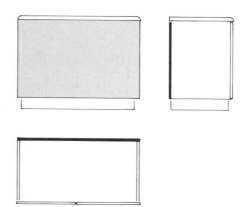

These shelves have been overloaded. The joints may also have become loose when the shelves were moved around: this is the disadvantage of having no back panel.

Based on the principle that the diagonals of a rectangle are of equal length, wires or pieces of strong string of equal length, when nailed or screwed diagonally onto a piece of furniture, straighten it and hold it at right angles again.
It is important to choose material that will not stretch, or to use wooden cleats.

A wooden cleat nailed on diagonally is very good for stabilizing shelves.
If the shelves are fairly full, e.g. with books, the batten will be inconspicuous.

A sheet of hardboard (painted or plastic coated) can be used as a back panel for part or for the whole of a piece of furniture. It is screwed or nailed to the sides and the shelves from behind. This is a simple and inexpensive solution. The back panel covers the wall of the room, and the shelves appear more solid with a back panel than without.

Flat metal plates can be screwed onto each corner to stabilize the shelves. When dealing with valuable furniture, a completely concealed construction is recommended.
The choice of which method to use depends on the quality of the material of the furniture, its use and its value to the owner.

Stabilizing furniture feet

Furniture is often wobbly because the feet are of different lengths or maybe even broken. To repair this, see the section 'Chairs: regulating height and the length of the legs'.
Loose components may also cause the furniture to wobble. In such cases repairs are fast and unproblematic.

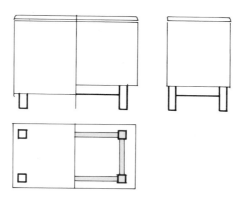

A stable, concealed joint can be made using dowels. Use at least two dowels per foot to prevent it from turning.
A dowelling jig or template simplifies the marking of the bore holes (see 'Dowel joints').

Screws into the feet have the same effect as dowels. They should not be positioned too close to the edge to prevent the wood from splitting. Boring pilot holes make the work easier and prevents splitting.
The screws cannot be seen when the door is closed. If these obstruct when the door is open, the screws can be sunk and filled.

The corner joints of stool-frame constructions receive a lot of wear. Dowels or tenons are the joints most often used here, but where the legs are slender they are often so short that they become loose.

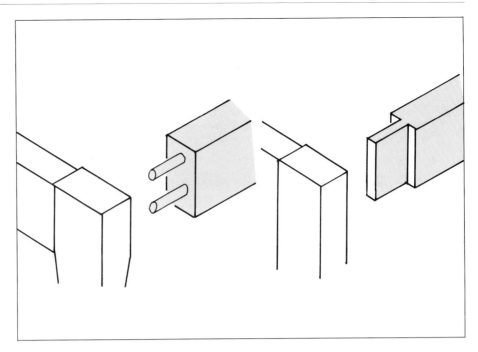

Loose legs can be re-glued. To do this, the joints have to be taken apart, the surfaces to be glued, cleaned up and then spread with a thin coat of glue. Lightly clamped, the leg is fitted into position; then the clamp is tightened.

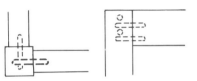

If new dowels are necessary, take care to set them at alternate heights, as shown in the diagram above.

Most stool-frame bases are only screwed to the carcases they support.
It is worthwhile removing the frame from the carcase during repairs so that you can work right up to the edges on all surfaces.

Drawers

Repairing fronts and bottoms

Drawers consist of a front, two sides, a back and a bottom panel.
Photos opposite: front pieces of solid wood are dovetailed at the corners. If this joint has become loose, the glued surfaces have to be cleaned up thoroughly and then glued again.
Use two clamps, not forgetting scrap wood, to press the components together.

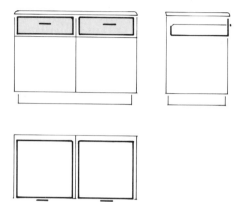

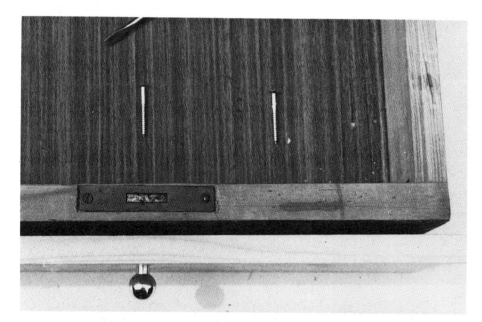

If a false front has become loose, it is screwed from inside the drawer. Special care must be taken that the front is in exactly the right position for the entire piece of furniture.

Bottom panels of solid wood are only found in old furniture. If there is a crack in the bottom panel, it can be pulled out of the grooves in the sides and glued. It is better to screw it onto the back rather than to nail it.

It is easy to replace old solid wooden panels with manufactured board, as long as they are of the same thickness. Antique furniture loses value due to such repairs, however, and it is easy to repair a piece of old furniture 'to death'.

Repairing Drawer runners

The traditional drawer has various pieces of wood, often part of the frame, which enable it to be opened smoothly and stably, and prevent it from tipping.

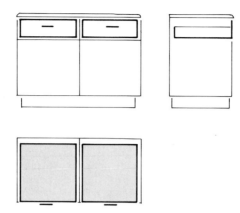

The guides keep it straight. They can become loose from warping or from constant use, and then the drawer can jam.

Use a batten to distribute the pressure of the clamp and glue the guide into position again. If there is not enough room for a clamp, the guide may have to be screwed, through the runner, and possibly from below.

The guides keep the drawer straight. Drawer kickers prevent it from tipping on opening. If a kicker is worn, the whole drawer is unsteady or tips.

Make a new kicker from hardwood cut to the same dimensions and bore pilot holes.
This block should extend almost to the front rail.

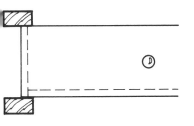

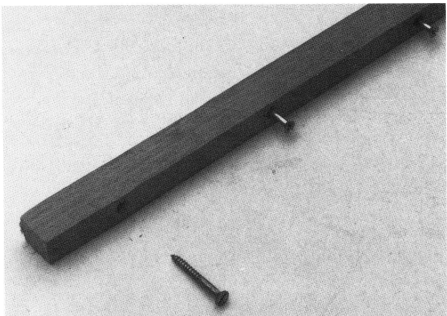

When screwing it into position make quite sure that the piece is horizontal.

When several drawers are on top of each other, the runner for one drawer also serves as the kicker for the drawer below.

Damaged knobs can only rarely be repaired. Having replacements specially turned is expensive; sometimes it is a good idea to put new knobs on one part of the furniture and replace them gradually.

Assembling roll tops and glueing battens

Roll tops consist of wooden battens running in grooves. The battens have a band of hessian or canvas glued to the back. This functions as a string of joints. The opened roll top, according to the type, is either rolled into a spiral at the bottom of the cupboard, or it runs along the back inside the cupboard.

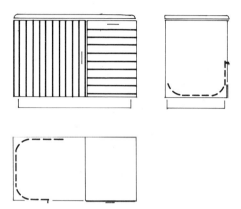

If the cloth is torn, first the roll top has to be taken out of the cupboard. There is usually an opening at the bottom or back where it can be removed.

If there is no such opening, it is easy to make one with a saw and a chisel. Cut an angle as close as possible to the groove, to prevent jamming. Then the roll top can be removed easily.

...anels are either fitted into grooves in ...e frame or in rebates and held in ...osition by beading.
...efore replacing panels, it is advisable to ...onsider whether or not to use a ...ifferent material, e.g. glass.

...f a panel is to be repaired or replaced, ...he groove can be chiselled open. Mark ...ut first, cutting lightly through the ...urface of the wood.

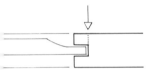

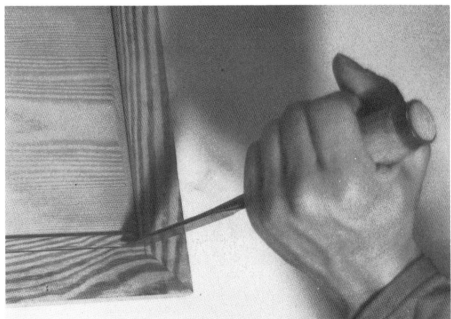

...Beading is nailed in to hold the new or ...epaired panels in place.

...The beading here is rebated, i.e. it fits ...over the edge of the frame – which gives ...a neat fit. Doors can also be panelled, ...e.g. by adding battens or sheets of ...plywood. It is also possible to fit in ...panels if two strips of beading are used ...nstead of one.

Fitting single and continuous hinges

Hinges are fittings used to attach a door or flap to a piece of furniture so that it can be moved. They are available as:
a) single hinges, e.g. sprung concealed hinge, butt hinge, pivot hinge
b) continuous hinges, e.g. piano hinge.
Some types of hinge allow the door to be lifted off.

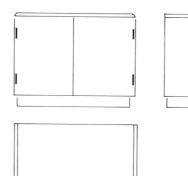

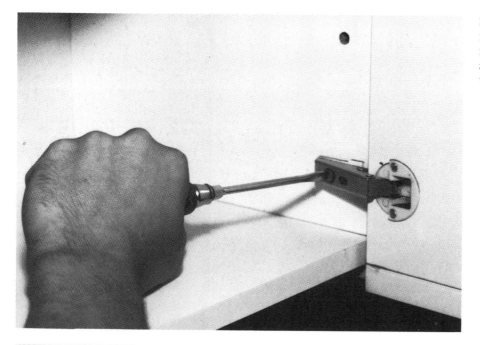

Sprung concealed hinges are most often found in kitchen cupboards. They are mounted inside the carcase. They are adjustable even after assembly, so doors which are not true can be readjusted.

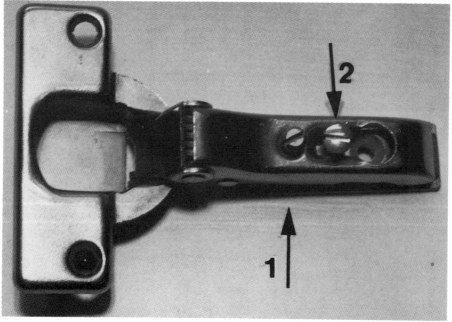

Screw 1 is used to adjust sideways, screw 2 to adjust the door forwards or backwards. The height cannot be adjusted.
A screwdriver of the correct size should be used to adjust the screws, as chewed up screw heads only make the damage worse.

A continuous or piano hinge can be strained if it is used too often or incorrectly, and the door will then hang at the wrong angle. To repair this the hinge first has to be unscrewed from the inside.
Before the hinge is screwed back into position, however, it should be checked to see whether it is bent or worn out, in which case a replacement is essential.

Using a chisel, split small pieces from a piece of solid wood. They should be big enough to be glued and hammered tightly into the holes from which the screws have been removed.

Fill all the holes in the door and carcase in this way. When the glue has dried, cut off the projecting ends of the pins. Now the hinge can be screwed on again.

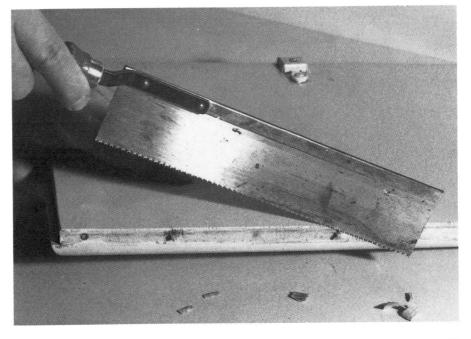

Removing and repairing pivot hinged doors

The pivot-type hinge is a very old way of fixing a door to a carcase. Doors used to be fitted this way and many flaps too. Pivot hinges cannot be seen from the front of the furniture as the parts of the hinge are recessed into the door and the carcase.

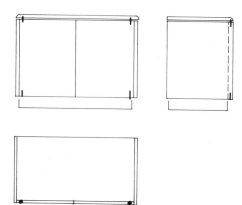

If a pivot has been broken out the door will hang at the wrong angle.
To repair this, first take out the door.

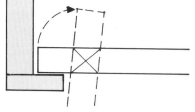

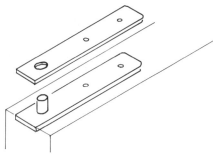

Do this by unscrewing the plate at the bottom of the door. This is the part with the pivot (see diagram above).
It is best to lie the cupboard on its back for this. The concealed hinge can be seen clearly when the door is open.

Now the door can be pulled out from below and then lifted right out of the top hinge. The photo shows the door seen from below, with the cupboard lying on its back.

Give cracked wood and loose joints a thin coat of glue. Do not forget to put pieces of scrap wood between the clamps and the piece to be glued. It is advisable to put pieces of paper between the scrap wood and the furniture to prevent them sticking together. If it does become stuck, the paper will tear and the pieces can later be removed with warm water.

If the screw holes are worn they can be filled with small wooden pins then glued. The top of the door is fitted back into the cupboard, then the bottom part fitted into the pivot hole and screwed tight.

Fitting and improving bolts and locks

Locks and bolts are used to keep doors, flaps and drawers closed, to prevent them opening by themselves or being opened by someone who shouldn't. If locked furniture is opened by force for any reason, there is generally some damage done to the wood. Similar damage is caused by wear or constant use.

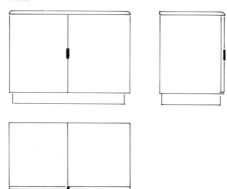

In some furniture there is only a hole in the base to take a bolt. The hole often frays at the edges, which looks ugly and no longer holds the bolt firmly.

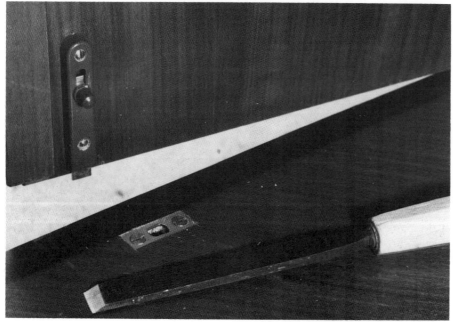

Use a chisel to fit a locking plate flush with the bottom of the cupboard and screw it tight.

The result is a neat hole for the bolt to fit into and the cupboard can be bolted firmly again.

Worn bolts are annoying. They can slip down and scratch the base of the cupboard. Sometimes the springs can be adjusted, but if not, the bolt should be replaced.

If cupboard doors with mortise locks are forced open, they will split or break. Remove the lock before glueing, open the broken part carefully to glue it, push the lock back loosely and then tighten the clamps.

Unfortunately some heyholes do look like the one in the photo on the right. Here we can mend and improve a lot with only a little effort. The scratches in the varnish disappear when a little clear varnish is applied.

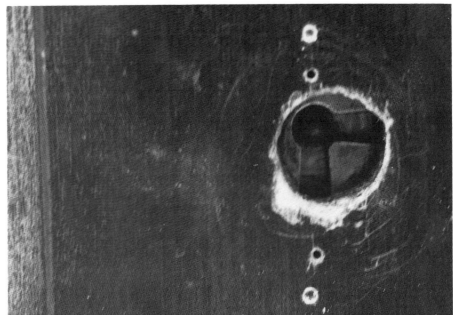

Nail or screw a escutcheons over the frayed keyhole.
There are some very nice, inexpensive escutcheons available, to suit all types of furniture. They not only mend but also improve the furniture.

Chairs

Regulating chair height and leg length

Wobbly chairs and tables are a great cause of annoyance. The repairs shown here can be used for all stool-frame constructions. Surface treatment is generally necessary afterwards.

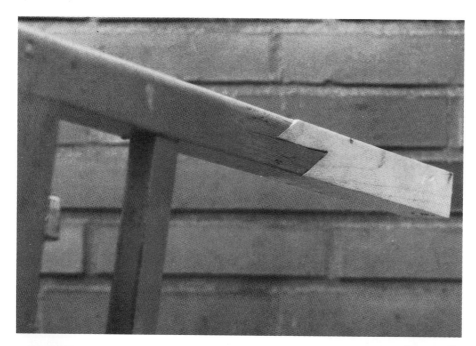

If a chair leg is badly damaged or broken, a new piece must be fitted. First the broken leg is sawn to the shape shown in the photo.

Shape the replacement piece with a saw and chisel to fit into the leg, with the grain running in the same direction. Do not cut the leg to the right length until it has been glued. A flush-fitting shape can be cut by clamping the leg to the new piece and sawing along the edges. Finally the leg is smoothed and sanded.

If the damaged part is very close to the end of the leg, saw it off and replace it with a straight piece.

To regulate the height of the chair, turn it upside down and place a batten with parallel sides across two legs. Now the length of the other legs can be gauged and any difference noticed.

Cut a piece of wood, preferably plywood, to the correct size and shape, glue it to the end of the leg first and then nail it with two thin tacks.
If using solid wood, first blunt the ends of the tacks by giving them a tap with a hammer on the tips. This prevents the wood splitting. Boring pilot holes for the nails has the same effect.

Fixing chair seats and frames

Frames and legs are joined by dowels or tenon joints. The seat is often only glued onto the frame, so that it is necessary to have the seat re-fitted when repair work has been done to the frame.

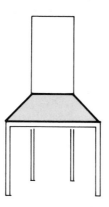

If tenon joints are loose, first the dirt and old glue have to be cleaned from the mortise and tenon. Then a new coat of glue can be applied. Sometimes the loosening of the joints is dependent on the seat being glued to the frame. Often enough this is the key to the stability of the whole frame.

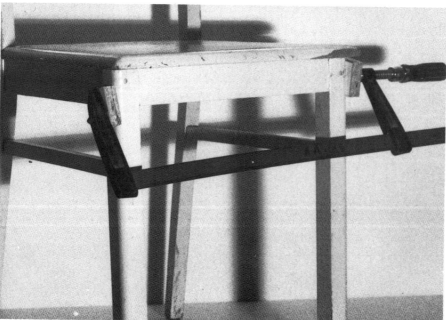

If the mortise is worn or the tenon broken, make a replacement tenon for the mortise and glue it into position. Cut off the tenon at its base. When both pieces are level, the components can be dowelled.

The seat also serves to add stability to the frame construction. A badly fitting seat may therefore cause the chair to wobble.

An effective reinforcement to the seat and the frame can be made by glueing and nailing or screwing wooden blocks to the bottom of the seat and the inside of the frame.

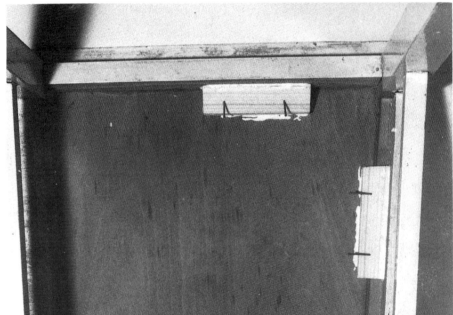

The corner joint can be reinforced by glueing wooden corner blocks onto the frame. An exact fit is just as important as the glueing of the surfaces. By cutting out two corners diagonally into the block and boring pilot holes, the block can also be screwed. With the block cut like this, the screws fit well and can press the glued surfaces together effectively.

Fixing table tops

Nowadays table tops usually consist of manufactured board covered with a great variety of surfaces. Old tables always had tops of solid wood. The legs and rails form the frame on which the top is fixed.

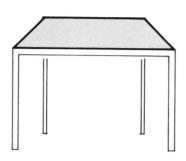

The top of this old kitchen table consists of battens of solid wood joined by mortise and tenon joints, between two end battens, also joined by mortise and tenons. Due to shrinkage large gaps have appeared between the boards.

Plane strips of wood to the exact size required, coat them thinly with glue and press them into the gaps. If hammering is necessary, you must place scrap wood above the strips. Finally plane off any wood still protruding until the surface is smooth. If the wood is to be left untreated, the correct choice of wood should be made beforehand. Sap and heart wood are different colours and the grain may show different patterns.

Wood buttons can be used to join a solid table top to the rails and they allow for wood movement.

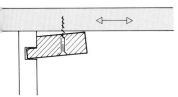

Cut a rebate into the rail leaving a space between the block and the top (see diagram). When chiselling the rebate, take care not to cut through the rail.

Bore a pilot hole in the button and glue it to the underside of the top. The screw pulls the top tightly against the rail, but the top is able to move against the grain. However, making wood buttons takes time and effort, and there are metal plates available which serve the same purpose.

Repairing bed sides and joints

As a rule beds are frame constructions that can be taken apart, i.e. the head and foot are joined to the sides by metal fittings. Hooks and sockets are most often found, but sometimes screws are used. The sides of the beds serve to hold the spring frame.

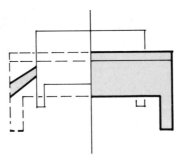

Single hooks, screwed into the sides of a bed, may become loose, fall out or break off.

First fill in a hole that has become too big by spreading some glue and driving in a pointed piece of wood. When the glue is dry, cut off the protruding piece, bore a small pilot hole and screw the hook back in at the correct height.

Sometimes an old spring frame has to be replaced. Very often the new one is narrower and therefore does not fit securely.

A new support can be made by screwing a wide batten to the inside of the bed side. Bore pilot holes and use largish screws, fairly close to each other.

The battens may also be attached to the sides with iron plates. These are also useful for attaching loose supports to the bed sides again.

It is often difficult to find new parts of the correct size for old beds. In such a case it may be advisable to buy a new bed. But what can be done with the old furniture? There are some suggestions for this in the fourth chapter on the topic of re-using old furniture.

Fitting seats

A panel of wood should be fitted into a
finished frame in stages, especially if the
shape is not rectangular and the sides
are of different lengths.

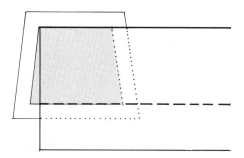

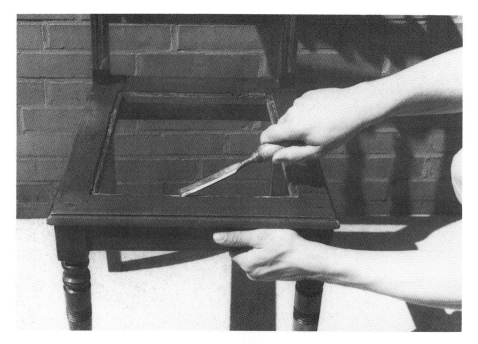

The damaged wicker seat has been
removed from this chair, to be replaced
by a plywood board. To do this, first
trim the rebate.

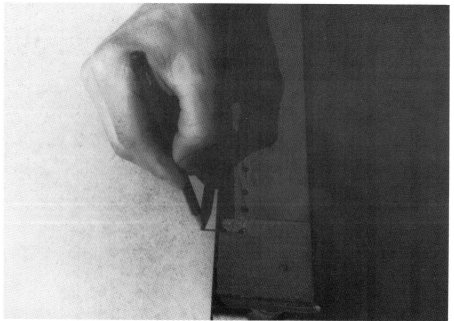

Place the plywood board along one of
the parallel sides, mark the depth of the
seat against the other parallel side, then
cut it out.
It is possible to work directly on the
chair, but it is better to have the board
held firmly in a vice when sawing.

Position the cut board on the chair and use a batten or ruler to mark a line on it parallel to the side to the frame.

If this angle is not cut quite correctly, it must be put right immediately. Only then can the new seat be put into position and the fourth side marked from one corner point to the other.

When the seat fits exactly, lightly sand the edges to prevent fraying or splintering. Then glue the seat and fit it into the rebate.
The surface work on the seat must be considered before fitting it. If necessary it must be treated, coated or upholstered before fitting.

Repairing edges

Edges are open to much accidental damage which often causes unsightly marks. However it is no problem for the skilled amateur furniture restorer to make repairs on solid wood edges.
For veneered edges, see section 'Fixing veneers; edges'.

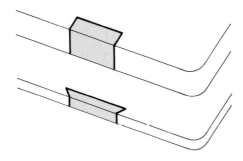

Heavy damage to a solid edge cannot be repaired by surface treatment. Here a new piece has to be inserted.

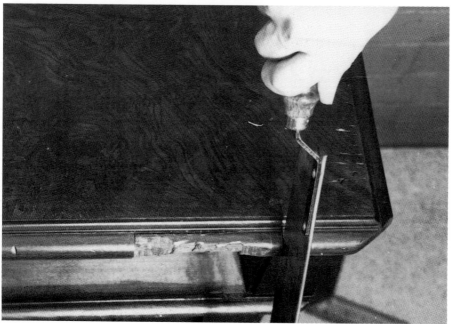

Use a backsaw to cut into the damaged edge to the right and left of the piece to be replaced. The cuts must be exactly vertical to be of the same depth at the top and bottom. The replacement can be inserted from the front, from above or from below, as shown in the diagram above.
The first method may be less conspicuous, while the second is longer lasting.

Remove the damaged wood with a chisel and mallet parallel to the furniture edge. Trim to a straight, smooth surface.

Cut a piece of wood to the correct size, choosing a piece of the same type and with the same grain as the rest of the edge. Then glue in the piece.

Plane smooth, and finish by sanding. Finally coat it with varnish of the same tone as the rest of the piece. It is always better to give a final coat to the whole of the edge rather than just the insert as this is then less conspicuous.

Strengthening shelves or boards

It is necessary to strengthen shelves or tops if their load causes them to sag or if solid wood warps.

Chipboard shelves can be strengthened by glueing a narrow board of the same material at the edge beneath the front edge. If necessary fix an edging strip.

Solid wood shelves can be reinforced with battens of solid wood. Glued at the edge beneath the shelf would give maximum strength, but such broad projections are not always desired, or even possible, due to the space they take up.

It is best to use clamps from the ends of the shelves and not from the middle. In this way battens that are not quite straight can be joined to the shelves in a straight line.

Boards made of butt-jointed battens of solid wood can warp due to changes in humidity. Before the days of manufactured materials such boards were kept straight by battens across each end, as drawing boards still are.

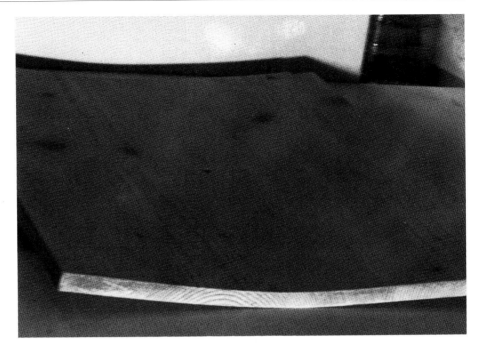

A batten screwed underneath the board straightens and stabilizes it. The surface area is now level. The wood must still be able to move, however, i.e. swell and shrink. This is a technical and physical necessity.

Slots in the battens allow for wood movement and thus prevent splitting. Although the battens are screwed on relatively tightly, the strength of the solid wood is so great that a slot in at least one end of the battens is necessary.

Removing dents and scratches

Unpolished softwoods such as pine are easily dented. Scratches can hardly be avoided on veneered or varnished surfaces.

If the damage is not too great it can be repaired quickly and easily.

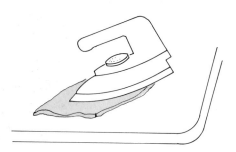

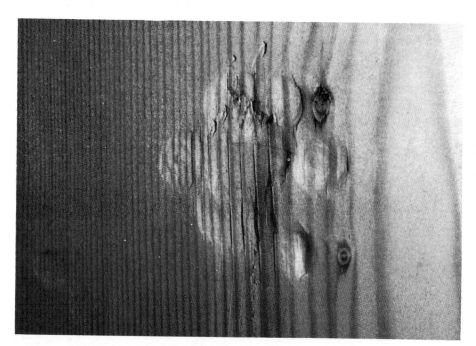

When solid wood surfaces are dented, the wood fibres are compressed. No actual material is lost, only the volume is affected. The fibres have to be expanded again.

Compressed wood fibres can be expanded by treatment with damp. Damp paper can be put on the dented place, which is advisable when the damage is fresh. If the dents are older, treatment with steam is recommended.

Cover the dent with a damp cloth and press a hot iron against it. This causes the wood fibres to expand. When the wood is dry it must be sanded.

The process can be repeated if necessary.

Shallow scratches in varnish disappear when coated with clear varnish.

Small cracks and deeper scratches can be evened out by rubbing with fine steel wool.

Fill deep cracks with wax or filler, available in various tones. Even shoe polish can have a good effect.

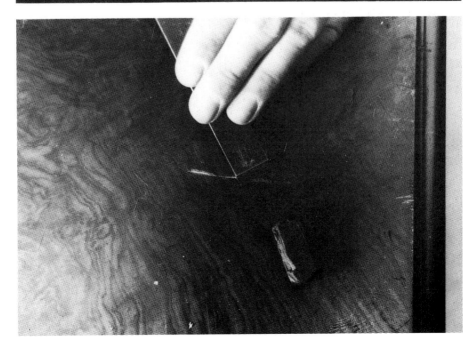

Removing burn and water marks

Once a piece of furniture has been repaired, the main problem is to find the right colour for the surface, and this needs practice. Stains can be mixed, but the tone changes when they dry or are varnished later. It is sensible to try out a colour on a part of the furniture that cannot be seen.

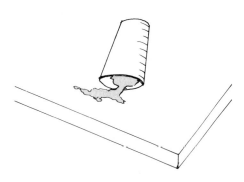

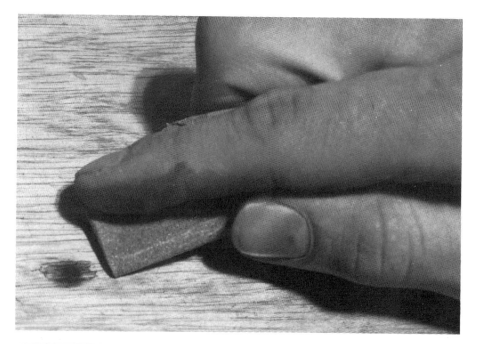

With burn marks on a flat surface, e.g. caused by cigarettes, rub down with sand paper until the dark mark does not show up any more.

Small marks can be painted over with water colours or oil paints, mixed to obtain the exact shade required. Afterwards treat the surface with clear varnish. It is easiest to spray this, and better to spray several thin coats rather than one thick one.

Water can leave unsightly marks on furniture. It is advisable to treat the whole surface to prevent edges forming.

First rub off the varnish with glass-paper in the direction of the grain and without using too much pressure.

Coat the surface with a suitable stain, using a little more on the damaged area. On vertical surfaces, e.g. cupboard sides, begin from the bottom, so that any drips will fall onto the damp surface and not show up later. When the stain is quite dry, spray with clear varnish.

Fixing veneer edges

The easiest way to repair edges is to use a veneer, since there are self-adhesive edging strips available in various types of wood.

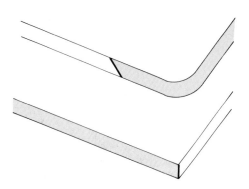

For repairing veneers the following tools are necessary:
For measuring and marking out
● try-square
● pencil
● carpet or trimming knife
● sliding bevel

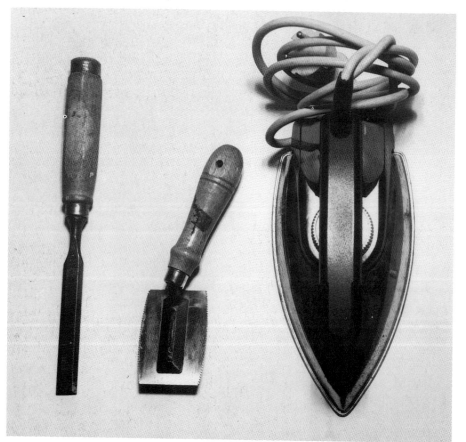

For removing veneer and cutting
● chisel
● veneer saw
● electric iron
● plane
An electric iron is ideal for fitting a veneer edge: first, every household has one; second, the heat can be set and stays at the same temperature; and third, it has a smooth surface for ironing on the veneer.

In order to give an edge a new veneer, choose a strip of self-adhesive edging that is slightly wider than the edge itself. Hold it flush against one of the edges and press a warm (not hot) iron along it until it sticks firmly.

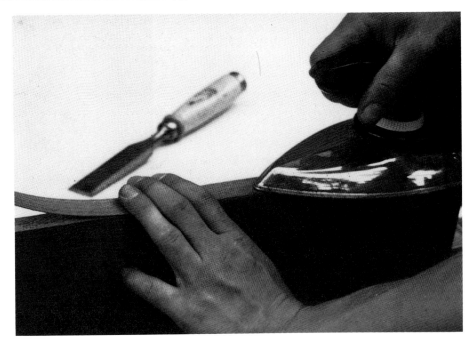

Afterwards go along the edge again pressing firmly with a cork block. Any air bubbles in a veneer can be removed in this way by warmth or pressure. A cork block is essential if the edges are to be worked properly, even if they are only narrow. A block can be made from a wooden block with cork on one side.

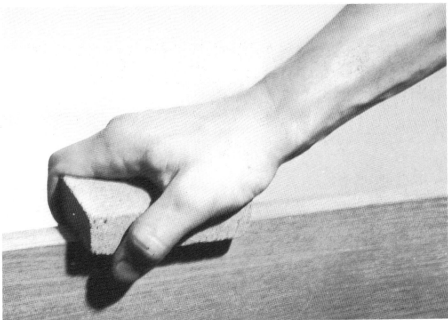

Finally remove the overlap by the use of a chisel, taking care not to damage the edge.

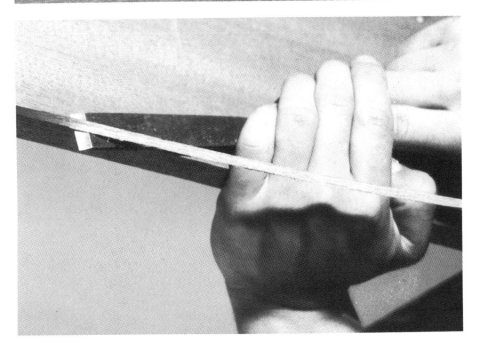

Restoring veneer surfaces

This is somewhat more difficult than veneering edges but the furniture restorer can make small repairs to veneered surfaces.

Air bubbles that do not disappear when a warm iron is applied must be slit open along the whole length. Apply some glue and weigh the spot down.

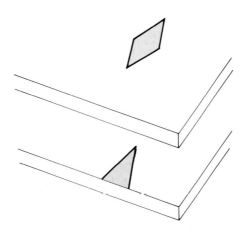

When there is a large damaged area a whole piece must be replaced. Mark out a diamond shape around the damaged area, or a triangle if it is at the edge, with the point in the direction of the veneer.

Fix a guide for the veneer saw (here a strip of wood is held by a clamp) and cut into the veneer along the mark. However, it is hardly worth buying a veneer saw for one repair job. A saw knife will have the same effect. It is easy to make one by filing teeth into an old knife with a triangular file and sharpening it.

To remove the old veneer, cover it with a damp cloth and press a warm iron against it for about a minute. The old veneer can then be removed with a chisel.

Try the new veneer for size, making sure that the grain fits in with the rest. If the shape to be fitted is complicated, cut a trial shape out of paper first.

Now glue in the new veneer. When the glue is dry, smooth the join with glasspaper. Before treating the surface, lightly sand the old veneer alongside the new piece.

4 Breathing new life into old furniture

KLAUS PRACHT · ILSE SCHAARSCHMIDT

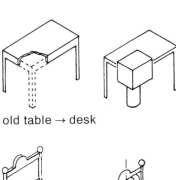

old table → desk

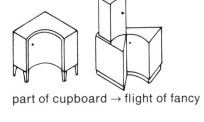

part of cupboard → flight of fancy

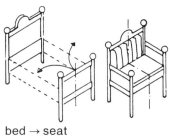

bed → seat

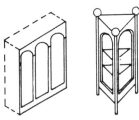

cupboard doors → display cabinet

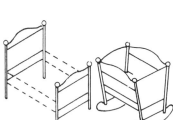

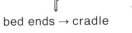

bed ends → cradle

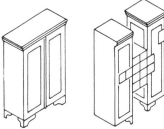

kitchen cupboard → crockery cupboard

Introduction

While it is always worthwhile trying to maintain old furniture, often it is in such a bad condition that repairwork would be too expensive. Such furniture is then usually thrown away and lost for ever. However, more and more people, particularly young people, like to make some use of old pieces of furniture, and redesigning old furniture is now in vogue. Chairs are made into tables, beds into benches, and cupboard doors into display cabinets!

In the first part of this chapter we offer various ideas and suggestions for reusing furniture or furniture parts. The second part contains general tips for improving the appearance of plain box constructions that are still usable but uninteresting to look at.

It is easiest to develop ideas for improving furniture using models. They can be made of paper or cardboard and allow all sorts of variations to be tried out. The results are sometimes astonishing.

This sort of improvement and redesigning can be carried out by the amateur woodworker, and the last part of the chapter gives detailed, practical tips on how to do so.

Old furniture – new function

Old chair backs, screwed together to form an arc, were joined with two chair bases to form the base of a coffee table. The colour of the chairs played an important role in this design. The designer has succeeded in alienating the individual chair parts, which emphasizes their new use.
(Design FH Hanover, Dept. of Art and Design. Students: Heike Buddenberg, Rolf Niehoff, Andrea Budzinski)

From chair to table

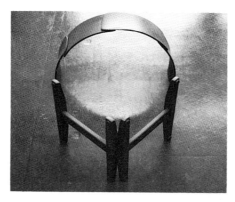

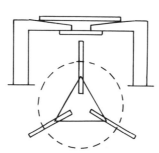

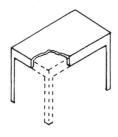 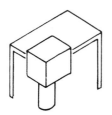

From kitchen table to writing desk

An old table with one leg and the top missing was the basis for this design. It was decided not to repair the table by reconstructing it as it was, as this would only have been an imitation.

An old kitchen table was turned into a desk. A rectangular piece was cut out of the table top, and a box construction standing on a pillar was added. The box construction is closed on all sides.

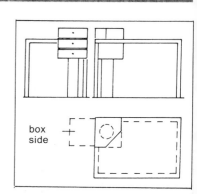

box side

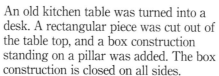

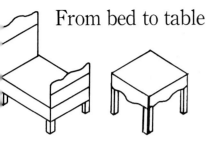

From bed to table

This coffee table has an unusual shape due to the use of parts of a bedstead. The legs were turned and some of the side rails curved: these were turned upside down to support the table top. (Design: Gabriele Reichmann)

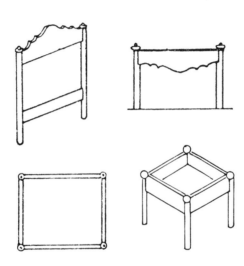

It is also possible to make a show table out of a bedstead. Instead of a wooden table top, a piece of glass is positioned on the frame in such a way that it can easily be lifted off.

Thus the items on display can be quickly changed. The show case is also very attractive when decorated with plastic film.

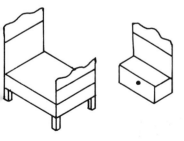

This shelf was made from a bedhead and parts of the bed rails. It could be used for a telephone, for example. (Design FH Hanover, Dept. of Art and Design. Students: Andrea Sievert and Bodo Dreier)

From bed to shelf

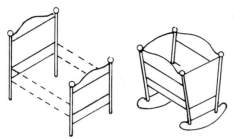

From bed to cradle

Old bedends were refunctioned as a cradle. The bed rails had been lost and the legs of the bedends cut off at the bottom. The bedends were wide enough to make a cradle, so only the height had to be changed a little.
The panels were cut shorter and the frame was given new dowels.
(Design: Klaus Pracht, production: Ralf Gilge)

In the diagram:

foot | head

bed ends used as sides of cradle

new parts

hooks allow construction to be taken apart

The photos show how the cradle can be taken apart and the workmanship of the individual elements. The new cradle 'head' is curved, which distinguishes it from the foot. The cradle is assembled using simple bed hooks, which allows it to be taken apart and stored when not in use.

For reasons of design all the new parts contrasted with the old ones. The colour of the ash contrasts with the new parts which were coated in light-coloured paint. Any final decoration can be added according to taste.

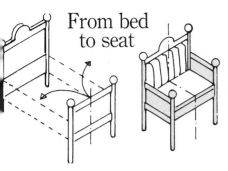

From bed to seat

A cushioned seat was made from a pair of very nicely shaped bedends. The bedends, with turned posts and mahogany veneer, were too good to throw away. The low foot was cut up the middle, and the resulting two parts used as the sides of the seat. (Design: Klaus Pracht)

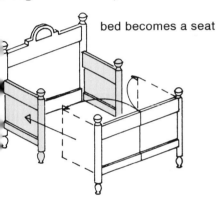

bed becomes a seat

This triangular seat was made from bedends. The ends were shortened so that the seat was not too deep for comfort. There is only one bed leg at the back. The fourth leg is used as the front rail beneath the seat.

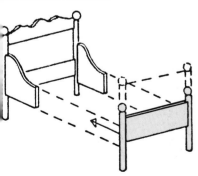

A bench with a box beneath the seat was made from a rustic spruce bedstead. The bedhead was used as the back of the bench, and parts of the side rails as the arms. The foot of the bed, shortened, was used as the front rail and feet. Part of the seat can be lifted open.

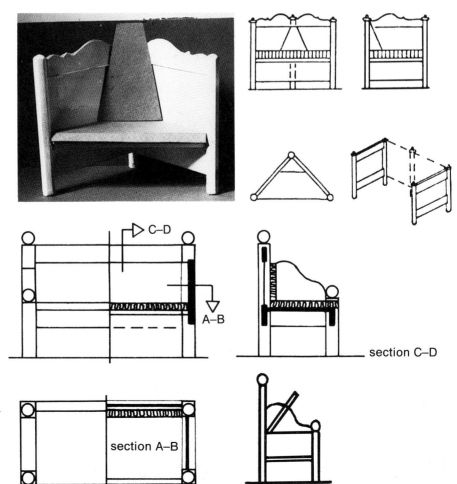

section C–D

section A–B

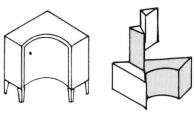

From cupboard parts to flight of fancy

The design of this corner cupboard with a curved door and shelves on both sides was no longer right for the owners, in particular because of the feet. We decided to rework the piece, as the material, ash veneer, was worth keeping.

Two designs were tried out on models. Both were based on keeping the curved front in conjunction with the angular sides, but removing the feet. The cupboard was made shallower and one side was cut away.
(Design: Clausen)

This design places the carcase flat against the wall and joins the extra triangular sections with a horizontal board.

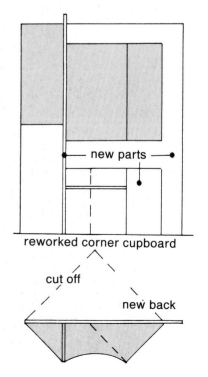

new parts

reworked corner cupboard

cut off

new back

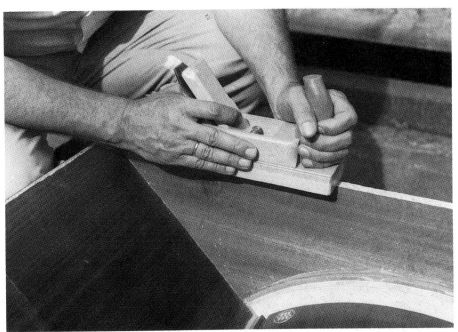

This second design was chosen because it was clearer and simpler. The old parts (white on the model) are set against each other and contrasting triangular shapes are added. Putting the design into practice created more ideas, as the photo below shows. The idea of standing the parts on each other stayed, but the top triangular box is no longer supported but suspended.

Without setting out to incorporate old pieces of furniture this object would hardly have been so unusual.
(Design: Thomas Pracht, Freiburg, Germany)

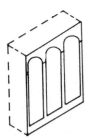

From cupboard doors to display cabinet

Well-designed cabinet doors are very rarely thrown away, even when the body of the cupboard has long since disappeared or been used as shelves etc. elsewhere.

Three glass cupboard doors were reworked here to make free-standing display cabinet. The use of broom handles to join them is a particularly original and simple idea. The broom sticks are screwed to the corners of the frame and stopped with putty. One of the doors stays movable and is hinged. (Design: Ralf Gilge)

It is often a shame to throw away old television sets which have a very well made wooden casing. An interesting idea was suggested for re-using the casing as a new, diagonally facing addition to a cabinet.

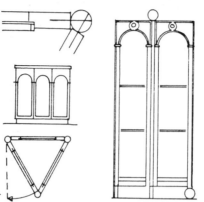
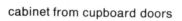

cabinet from cupboard doors

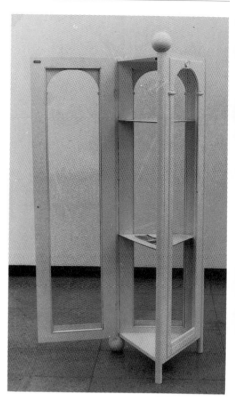

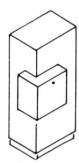

Adding pieces to existing furniture

Many small pieces of furniture are no longer used because the design of their feet or legs is out of fashion, e.g. conically shaped legs set at acute angles. Reworking such pieces tends – obviously – to result in the removal of these parts. The remaining parts can be mounted onto a wall or built into a cupboard, as shown here.

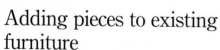

old cupboard

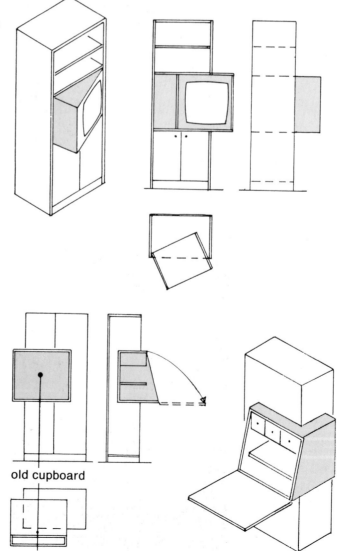

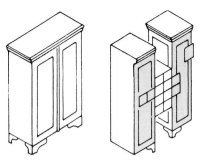

Interchanging cupboard halves

This old kitchen cupboard had been put into the attic and it was a challenge to find a new function for it. Restoration in the usual sense was not enough for the owner, who wanted the material kept, but a modern design.

The cupboard was cut vertically up the centre. With the sides interchanged, the front parts now look very decorative with the corner mouldings facing. The sides were filled in with boards placed in such a way that the surface of the old cupboard can still be seen. Nothing is concealed – every detail on the original cupboard has been saved.

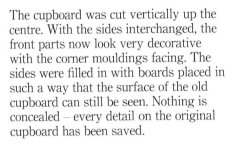

The doors were divided horizontally and given new hinges. An asymmetrical glass display case with bars joins the two old parts.
(Design: Klaus Pracht)

Sprucing up plain furniture

The examples we have looked at show how highly original ideas can be formed using the basic concept of reworking an old piece of furniture. There is an enormous variety of combinations of old and new parts. We deliberately avoided using the new parts inconspicuously, as the result would have lacked excitement and resembled repairwork that unsuccessfully pretends to reconstruct the original.

Using new and old pieces together in contrast – material, form and colour – can create exciting combinations. The result is always an experience.
The ideas for enhancing plain pieces of furniture already in use are influenced by the quality of the material and depend on the designer's imagination. As an aid to imagination, I have given general hints on the next few pages.

A good starting point is to make a scale drawing of three sides of the piece of furniture. Depending on the actual size, a scale of 1:5, 1:10 or 1:20 is useful. Changes can be marked on transparent paper and tried out by holding it above the original drawing.

Another idea is to make paper models of the parts of furniture worth keeping. New ideas are easier to visualize on a model than on paper. A cupboard represented by a small white cube is easily turned around, but if, for example, only the door is worth keeping, a model of this can be tried against abstract shapes.

Using a model also offers the opportunity of trying out furniture in positions which do not obviously have anything to do with their function. The designer can choose from the many ideas created like this. A successful result is very uplifting.

Adding to furniture

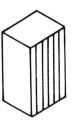 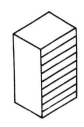 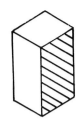

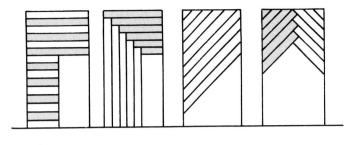

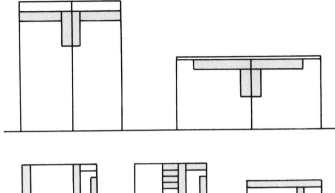

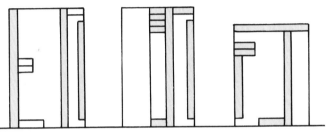

Sloping off corners

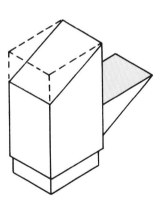 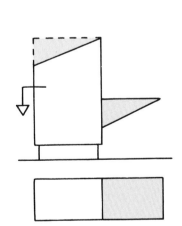

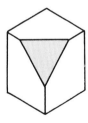 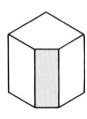

cutting off
a corner

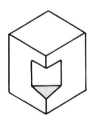 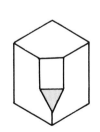

sloping off
part of
a corner

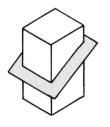 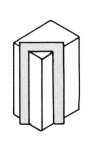 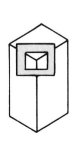

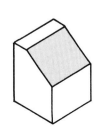 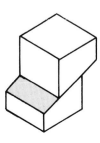

sloping off
side

125

Moving furniture angles

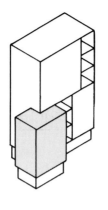
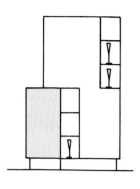

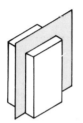
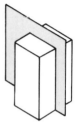
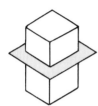

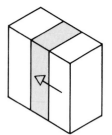

moving together

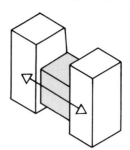

pulling apart

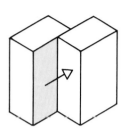

moving back

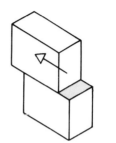

moving sideways

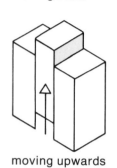

moving upwards

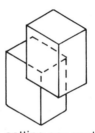

setting one part
inside another

Changing angles

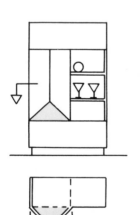
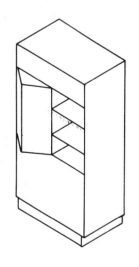

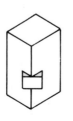

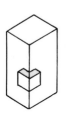

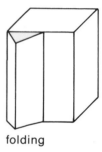

folding

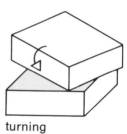

turning

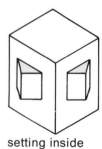

setting inside

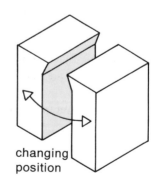

changing
position

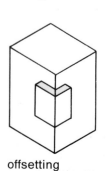

offsetting

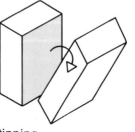

tipping

Techniques

The small diagram names the furniture parts and the sections.

In the larger sections the details illustrated below are marked.

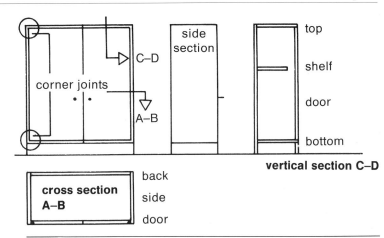

vertical section C–D

cross section A–B

back
side
door

Sections

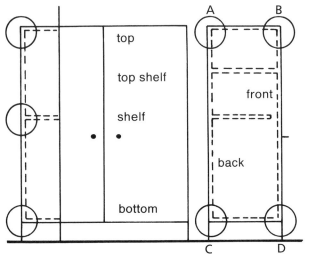

doors and hinges

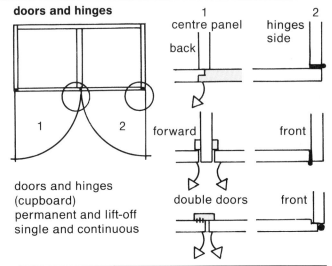

doors and hinges
(cupboard)
permanent and lift-off
single and continuous

1 centre panel
back
2 hinges side
forward
front
double doors
front

variations on the details A and B

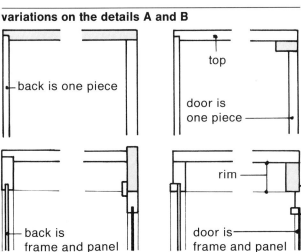

back is one piece

top

door is one piece

back is frame and panel

rim

door is frame and panel

bottom of central and side panels

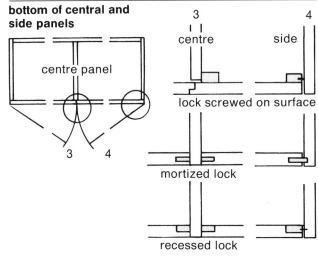

centre panel

3 centre
4 side
lock screwed on surface
mortized lock
recessed lock

variations on details C and D

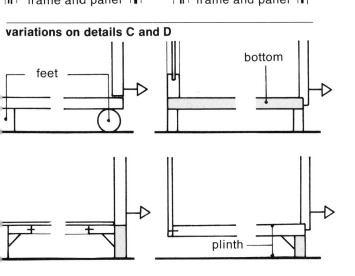

feet

bottom

plinth

back and sides

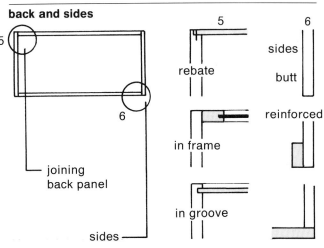

joining back panel

sides

5 rebate
6 sides butt
reinforced
in frame
in groove

Details

The variations on the details show a
variety of constructional possibilities.
The column on the right contains
suggestions for very simple ways of
reworking furniture using hardboard,
glue, nails and PVC foil.

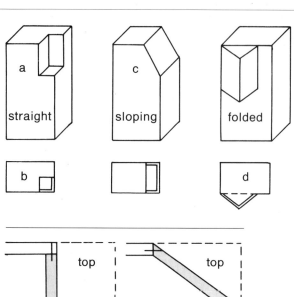

straight   sloping   folded

corner joints, permanent

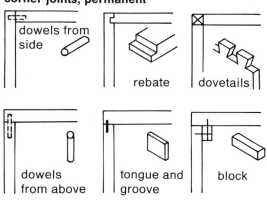

dowels from side

rebate   dovetails

dowels from above   tongue and groove   block

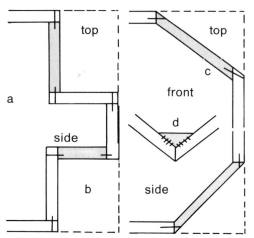

a   top   top

front

side   c

d

b   side

corner joints, knockdown fittings

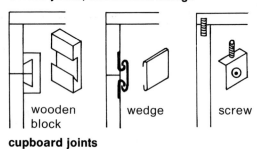

wooden block   wedge   screw

cupboard joints

carcase corners

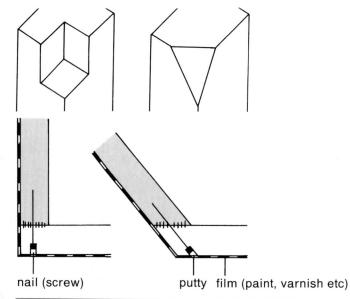

nail (screw)   putty film (paint, varnish etc)

shelves

single   set of shelves

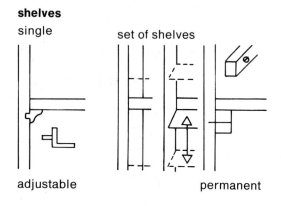

adjustable   permanent

triangular joints

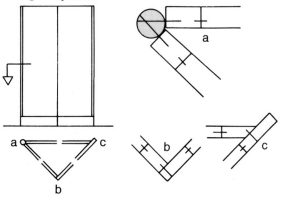

a   c   a

b   b   c